THE WALK
-THE-
WALK
BOOK

it's a God thing!

Other books in the Young Women of Faith Library

Young Women of Faith

THE WALK -THE- WALK BOOK

it's a God thing!

Written by Nancy Rue
Illustrated by Lyn Boyer

Zonderkidz

Zonder**kidz**.

The children's group of Zondervan

www.zonderkidz.com

The Walk-the-Walk Book
Copyright 2003 by Women of Faith

Requests for information should be addressed to:
Grand Rapids, Michigan 49530

Library of Congress Cataloging-in-Publication Data

Rue, Nancy N.
  The walk-the-walk book : it's a God thing! / written by Nancy Rue ;
illustrated by Lyn Boyer.
     p. cm.— (Young women of faith library)
  ISBN 0-310-70259-3 (pbk.)
  1. Girls—Religious life—Juvenile literature.   2. Christian life—Juvenile literature.
I. Boyer, Lyn.   II. Title.   III. Young women of faith.
BV4551.3.R84 2003
248.8'2—dc21

                                                                      2003000548

Published in association with the literary agency of Alive Communications, Inc., 7680 Goddard Street, Suite 200, Colorado Springs, CO 80920.

Editor: Barbara J. Scott
Art direction: Michelle Lenger
Interior design: Lyn Boyer

Printed in the United States of America

03 04 05 06 07 /❖DC/ 10 9 8 7 6 5 4 3 2 1

Contents

Discipline ... Doesn't That Mean You're Grounded?

My soul thirsts for God, for the living God.
When can I go and meet with God?
Psalm 42:2

Before you toss this book into the nearest corner and hightail it in the other direction because you just saw the word *discipline*—wait! It's not what you think!

Discipline probably brings a lot of less-than-wonderful images to mind— like being grounded when you skipped cleaning up your room after school to catch one more rerun of *Full House* on TV. Or having your telephone privileges taken away because your teacher sent home a note saying you weren't getting your homework done.

Or you may be thinking about getting the talking-to of your life from your parents because you got in trouble at school for passing notes to your best friend (even though you tried to explain how *important* that note was!).

Your list may be a little different. It may even be longer! But the point is that the word *discipline* probably has a bad meaning with girls your age. It sure isn't something you go looking for, right?

Here's the good news: that isn't the kind of discipline we're talking about here. (If you were looking for a book on how to *avoid* being disciplined by your parents, try *The Buddy Book* and *The It's MY Life Book!*). These disciplines—spiritual disciplines—are completely different. We're not talking about punishment; we're talking about *training*—the kind you opt for without anybody forcing you. It's the kind of training that you take on because of *all* these things:

- You want to be way close to God so you'll always know what to do.
- You don't want to be forced into doing something just because the "popular kids" are doing it.
- You want to be joyful most of the time (even when things aren't going so well).
- You want to be who God wants you to be.
- You want to be free to do what God wants you to do.

What does it look like to be that kind of person? Let's look at how each of the Girlz is practicing a spiritual discipline each day.

Lily has quiet time with God every day in her special place, which always includes prayer journaling and getting into the Bible for the stuff that's going to help her today. She doesn't realize it yet, but that's why she was able to control herself just yesterday. Ashley Adamson made one of her usual sarcastic remarks about Lily being a "study geek," but Lily didn't say, "Well, at least I'm not a study *loser* like you." She didn't even toss her head and stomp off. Lily just smiled and said, "And I'm *proud* of it, Ashley" and then walked away happy.

Reni has really de-cluttered her life, so she can now actually see the floor in her bedroom and she has more time and space for God in her life. Wednesday she would normally have gone to yet another violin lesson (she used to take five lessons a week so she could be the best player in the county). She was just about to dabble with her watercolors when the phone rang. It was Lily, crying her eyes out and needing a friend big-time. Reni had time to ask her over. And amazingly, there was a place for Lil to sit when she got there! Lily's tears were gone within five minutes.

Suzy, who as you know is way shy, has started volunteering for some service projects at church. First she served tables at the moms luncheon. When that was pretty cool, she joined a group that was going to Potter's House to hand out cookies to kids from homeless families. That actually turned out to be fun, so Suzy decided to do her own cookie handout for everybody in her class, at recess during January, when life can be pretty dull after Christmas. She's noticing that she feels less shy these days.

Zooey has recently started propping herself up on her pillows at night before she goes to sleep and talking to God about all the stuff she isn't proud of from her day. These are things like talking back to her mom, whispering "I hate you" when her brother was out of earshot, and feeling jealous of Lily because she got another role in a school play. She's learned to tell God all about the yuckiness, accept where she is right now, and pray for the help to move on with the determination to be better tomorrow. It's a funny thing. Zooey no longer comes home at the end of the day and flops on the couch to flip channels all evening. She can concentrate on getting her homework done. She can even enjoy going to the movies with the Girlz more—all because she is no longer constantly thinking, *If only I didn't have such a big mouth* or *If only I wasn't so hateful* and *If only I wasn't the laziest person on the planet.* Instead she's thinking, *I'm sorry, God. Will you help me do better next time?*

Kresha goes to church to worship every Sunday now. She sings louder, she laughs right out loud when the pastor makes a joke in the sermon, and she cries when a prayer seems to be just for her. But that isn't all. She has also started doing some worshiping on her own. She takes a long bath every Saturday night (in spite of her little brothers banging on the door) and prays that God will wash away her sins so she'll be ready to receive all the spiritual stuff that'll be coming to her in church the next day. She wears a cross every day, and as she puts it on, she prays for more and more faith. And when she realized God had helped her stop yelling at her little brothers (when they banged on the bathroom door), she threw a pizza party for herself and the Girlz—and God.

The Girlz say the results of these spiritual disciplines are awesome.

HOW IS THIS A God Thing?

On the night of the Last Supper, when Jesus was telling his disciples what was about to happen and why, he prayed for them. One of the things he said to his Father was, "I have brought you glory on earth by completing the work you gave me to do" (John 17:4).

And what God assigned him to do was pretty big. He had to show people exactly what God was like and then return to God by being crucified, dying, rising again, and then being lifted back up to heaven. Aren't you glad *we* don't have that assignment? How did Jesus do it?

The obvious answer is that it was easier for him because he was the Son of God—but it isn't that simple. He had to come to earth in human form and suffer through everything we have to suffer through in life. Since it was his job to show us how to get our own missions from God accomplished (and we all have them), he couldn't just snap his God fingers and make it happen. He had to demonstrate for us.

So what did he do to make it possible for him to really know God, hear him, and obey him? How did he resist the temptation to say, "Oh, forget it. I'm just going to perform a miracle and get it over with!"

Jesus practiced the same spiritual disciplines we're going to talk about in this book.

Quiet Time

In spite of how busy he was (he was always being followed around by crowds of people clamoring to have their sicknesses healed and asking endless questions), Jesus took a lot of time to be alone with God. He started off his whole ministry by spending forty days by himself in the desert (now *that's* a lot of alone time!), and after that he was constantly going off by himself to pray. He spent a whole night in prayer before he picked his disciples (Luke 6:12), and he went off in a boat by himself when he got the news that John the Baptist had been killed. He wasn't just trying to get away from people (whining little brothers, nagging moms, friends he was sick of). He just wanted to hear God better. We know that while he was alone, he *prayed* and *listened* and *devoted* himself to his Father, because every time he came out of solitude, he went right back to doing what God had sent him to do—healing, teaching, and forgiving people.

Simplicity

Jesus didn't clutter up his life with a lot of stuff that would distract him from his ministry, and he advised his disciples to follow his example. When he sent them out to spread the good news that the Son of God had arrived to teach people how to change their lives, he advised them to keep it simple. He told them not to load themselves down with equipment and stuff. He urged them not to stay in fancy hotels but rather to be content with someplace modest. He told them to just leave quietly if people didn't like them and didn't want to listen to their message (Luke 9:3–5). The disciples did what he said—following the example he was living for them— and they got great results! They spread the news and healed people everywhere they went, which was exactly what God wanted them to do.

Service

Although Jesus was the Son of God, he was constantly serving other people. He didn't mind getting his hands dirty to heal them (John 9:6). He went to his friends Mary and Martha and raised their brother, Lazarus, from the dead (John 11:38–44). And just so his disciples wouldn't think they could only serve by doing big, flashy things, he washed the gross, caked-on dirt from their feet (John 13:3–11). We're talking towel, apron, and the whole thing. When the disciples saw him do this, they realized that the way the world decides who is great and who isn't is a bunch of hogwash. They learned that all of us are equal in God's eyes and need to behave that way.

Confession

Jesus stayed true to his assignment throughout his ministry. He never doubted that he was doing the right thing or that he was doing it the right way. (Wouldn't *that* be a nice feeling?) But the night he was about to go to his death, he got pretty depressed. One of his dearest friends was about to turn him over to the authorities. He was about to be nailed to a cross. Even though he was the Son of God, he began to wonder if there could be another way to do what God wanted. Of course he knew there wasn't, but instead of hiding his doubt from

God, he went straight to his Father with his feelings. "Father," he said, "if you are willing, take this cup from me" (Luke 22:42). And what happened? God immediately took over and Jesus knew what was right. "Yet," he said right away, "not my will, but yours be done." Jesus' confession to God gave him the determination to go ahead with his assignment to die for us so we could give him all our sin and be forgiven and blessed.

Worship

Jesus went to the temple to worship every Sabbath. And he didn't just sit back and listen to the readings and the sermon. He participated in the worship. Half the time he took over! Remember when he spent the whole day teaching in the meeting place and blew everybody away with the way he taught the Scriptures (Mark 1:21-22)? And when he gave a lecture in the meeting place in his hometown (Mark 4:16-22)? Oh, and how about when he read the scroll of the prophet Isaiah and revealed that he was about to fulfill that prophecy (Luke 4:17–21)? Jesus knew how important it was for people to get together and encourage each other in their journeys with God. People began to know they could trust him, because he "belonged" with them. He was one of them.

Obviously, if Jesus practiced those disciplines—spending quiet time alone with God, living a simple life, serving other people, confessing to God, worshiping God—we're supposed to practice them, too.

But it isn't just a matter of doing it because we're supposed to. This isn't another bunch of things to add to your schedule and if you do them you'll go to heaven. We, like Jesus, need to do these things to get the same benefits Jesus did.

- We'll get to experience being Christians instead of just going to church and saying our prayers.
- We'll be changed into more complete, happier people.
- We'll be free from other people's opinions that weigh us down.
- We'll be close to God.

- We'll know what it is God wants us to do in our lives.

We can't get any of that good stuff just by trying. God gives us all that through a thing called *grace,* just because he loves us. But we have to show God we really want to be right in his eyes to get that grace, and we get it through the spiritual disciplines.

CHECK Yourself OUT

It could be that you're practicing some of the spiritual disciplines already and don't even know it! (That would be cool, wouldn't it?) Let's find out where you are right now and where you need to be—which is always a good way to start any journey.

In each set of statements, put a star next to the one that best fits you. If none of the statements fit you, put a star next to the one that says, "None of these statements sound like me." Be totally honest because there are no right or wrong, good or bad answers. You're looking for what's true for you right now.

Quiet Time

_____1. I have a special place where I like to go sometimes by myself, just to do nothing.

_____2. I sometimes go off by myself to pray.

_____3. I spend time alone every day, praying and writing in a journal and listening to God.

_____4. None of these statements sounds like me.

Simplicity

_____1. Sometimes I think I have too much stuff or too much to do or both.

_____2. Every once in a while I give some of my stuff away.

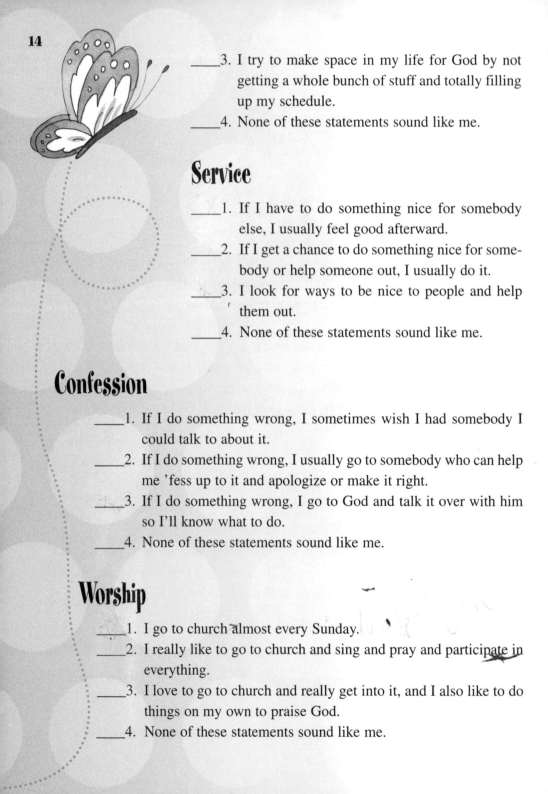

_____3. I try to make space in my life for God by not getting a whole bunch of stuff and totally filling up my schedule.

_____4. None of these statements sound like me.

Service

_____1. If I have to do something nice for somebody else, I usually feel good afterward.

_____2. If I get a chance to do something nice for somebody or help someone out, I usually do it.

_____3. I look for ways to be nice to people and help them out.

_____4. None of these statements sound like me.

Confession

_____1. If I do something wrong, I sometimes wish I had somebody I could talk to about it.

_____2. If I do something wrong, I usually go to somebody who can help me 'fess up to it and apologize or make it right.

_____3. If I do something wrong, I go to God and talk it over with him so I'll know what to do.

_____4. None of these statements sound like me.

Worship

_____1. I go to church almost every Sunday.

_____2. I really like to go to church and sing and pray and participate in everything.

_____3. I love to go to church and really get into it, and I also like to do things on my own to praise God.

_____4. None of these statements sound like me.

So what do your answers mean? Keep in mind that we're not telling you that you're the best—or the worst!—spiritually disciplined person in all Christianity. This is just a way for you to find out how much discipline you already have so God can work with you to give you all those spiritual goodies we've been talking about!

If most of your answers were number 1s, that means you have the right idea about spiritual discipline already. Look especially at the sets where you put a star next to number 1, so you can say to yourself, "Wow, I've already got it going on in that area." Once you learn more about each of those disciplines, you'll fall naturally into them. It'll almost be a piece of cake!

If most of your answers were number 2s, it tells you that you're already partly practicing those disciplines. Look especially closely at the sets where you put a star next to number 2, because those are the areas where you have a good start. Once you learn more about each of the disciplines, you'll see how you can become even closer to God.

If most of your answers were number 3s, you're there, at least in the sets where you put a star next to number 3. Look closely at the ones where you didn't, because those are the ones you'll want to work on. Our hope for you is that eventually you'll be practicing all the disciplines. That's going to be really cool for you and God.

If most of your answers were number 4s, you've probably had a lot of stuff competing for your attention. Now that you have a chance to learn more about spiritual disciplines and how to practice them, you'll be able to focus more and more of your attention on God—and that's a good thing. Of course you'll want to read this whole book and do the activities, but really get into the chapters about the disciplines where you had number 4 stars. Don't try to weave all the spiritual disciplines into your life at once. Take one at a time and don't move on to the next until you feel that discipline is such a part of your everyday activities that you wouldn't know what to do without it.

Just Do It

Before we start looking at the individual disciplines in the next five chapters, there are some things you can do to get ready. Note to remember: *This is not supposed to be just one more thing you have to do! This is a joyful thing, a good thing, something that's going to change your life—for the better!* So if completing this list of preparations drags you down, stop and pray that God will help you see the good part and fill you with the kind of excitement you feel when you're about to go to your first horseback riding class or make your first try at a new hairstyle, or anything else cool that you haven't done before.

Spiritual Discipline Preparation List

_____Tell an adult whose life with God you really respect that you are about to start the spiritual disciplines. Ask that person to pray for you, and ask if you can check in with him or her once in a while, just to talk about how it's going. Taking this journey means even more if you have someone to share it with.

_____Tell your mom or dad and ask for their support as you go along. We'll talk about what that means for each discipline a little later, but for now an example of how your parents could support you would be for them to help you find some privacy for your quiet times with God. It might help to have one of them read this book before you begin your journey.

_____If you don't already keep a journal, now would be a good time to get one and decorate it to look like *you*. That way, as you go along your discipline path, you can write down the amazing things that happen. You'll want to jot down when a prayer is answered. You'll probably have the urge to write all about the service project you did and maybe put in some pictures. Who knows? You might even be inspired by a worship service to write your own praise song or prayer.

_____Start to pray, right now, that you will become so spiritually disciplined that God will never feel more than a breath away from you. If you're not sure where to start, the "Talking to God About It" section of this chapter will help.

Girlz WANT TO KNOW

Still a little unsure about this whole spiritual disciplines thing? So were the Girlz. Maybe our answers to them will help you too.

✿ *ZOEY: I just started going to church with my friends, and my mother already thinks I'm going too far with "all that church stuff." Would it be better for me to just go to church and not mess things up?*

You definitely have to honor your mom, Zooey. In this case that means respecting her opinion and not throwing yours in her face constantly. And you definitely don't want to find yourself being forbidden to go to church at all because you've "gone too far." But that doesn't mean you can't practice the disciplines. You don't have to make a big deal out of having quiet time with God. In fact, as you'll learn, that's the whole point of doing it—that it's private. You don't have to announce twenty times that you're cleaning out your closet to make space in your life for God. Just do it. Do you get the idea? It isn't a matter of "sneaking around."

Your relationship with God is between you and him, not between you and your mom, so develop it quietly. Chances are, your mom is going to see the changes in you—and that could be the start of some talks that might make your mom want to know more about what you're doing. It's cool how God works that way.

✿ *KRESHA: There is no way I'm going to get to do any of this without my little brothers getting into it and ruining it, like always. It's going to take a lot of spiritual discipline just to keep me from smacking them when they start looking between my mattresses for my journal—which they definitely will! What can I do?*

Before you start chasing after them with a whip, relax. Who says your brothers have to know anything about your spiritual disciplines? Who invited them? You can have alone time when they've gone to bed (they do sleep, don't they?) or before they get up in the morning. When you offer to walk an elderly neighbor's dog for free, don't broadcast it at the dinner table. And when you mess up, confess it to your youth pastor, not to them! When your brothers are ready, they might want to learn about spiritual disciplines themselves. But for right now, it's your little secret.

✿ *RENI: I already have violin lessons, school and city orchestra, plus Girlz Only Club and church stuff. I don't have time to do anything else, unless I quit doing homework, which my parents would just love.*

You don't have to give up homework (bummer, huh?) to practice the spiritual disciplines, Reni. You might not even have to give up any of your other activities either. This isn't "one more thing" to add to your schedule. This is something you'll weave into your everyday life. Soon it will be as natural as taking time out to eat and sleep and take a bath and talk on the phone to your friends. You wouldn't miss a meal, and you won't miss a quiet time once you've learned to treasure it. You'd die before you'd skip saying hi to your friends at school. Soon it'll be just as important for you to say hi to the kids who always get left out. Get the idea?

Before long the spiritual disciplines won't be something you *do;* they'll be the way you *live.* At some point you might even let one or two of your after-school activities go because being close to God is more important to you than anything else. Doing the God thing makes everything else you do so much better.

Talking to God About It

Dear _____ (*your favorite way of address-ing God*),

I'm about to start some spiritual disciplines, and I need your help. (Duh, huh? When don't I need your help?)

According to my "Check Yourself Out" quiz, some of the disciplines are going to be harder for me than others—the ones where I starred number 4s. Those would be _____.
I'm going to need your extra-special help with those.

I'm also concerned about the things on this list that I've put check marks by:

_____*not sticking with it*
_____*not understanding how to do it*

_____*not having time to do it*

_____*not having a place to do it*

_____*not having a chance to do it, because no opportunities come up*

_____*not having anybody I can talk to about it*

_____*not getting close to you no matter how hard I try*

One thing I know for sure: if I even try to practice these disciplines in my life, you'll be here with me, helping me become the person you want me to be. It sounds so good, God—please make it so!

I love you more than anything.

Amen.

Being really close to God would be like . . .

Time Alone for You and God

Very early in the morning, while it was still dark, Jesus got up, left the house and went off to a solitary place, where he prayed.
Mark 1:35

Lily has no trouble making the spiritual discipline of quiet time part of her routine. She loves to be by herself, with nobody in her face, where she's free to think her own thoughts and be what Ashley and her crew would call "so weird." She enjoys praying, writing in her journal, and thinking about God. Most of the time she can't *wait* to get through her homework so she and her dog Otto can curl up next to her big stuffed panda, China, and snuggle in with God.

It's taken some time for **Reni** and **Suzy** to really get into it. At first when Reni sat down to pray and read her Bible, she got restless, thinking about all the other things she needed to do—like practice her violin and do the homework she didn't get to finish because she was at orchestra practice. Besides, Reni's a social bug. She'd much rather be doing quiet time on the phone! That's not a problem for Suzy. She's naturally quiet and likes to be by herself. But once she settled in with her journal and Bible, she started to panic. This was time with *God,* for Pete's sake! What if she did it *wrong?* Wouldn't that be worse than not doing it at all?

Zooey gave up after the first couple of tries. She had no idea what to write in a journal (she evidently hasn't read *The Creativity Book*!), and when she opened the Bible to Genesis 1:1, she didn't understand a thing she read. She felt bad about thinking that being with God was pretty boring, but after those first few sessions she just couldn't stick with it.

And **Kresha**? Bless her heart, she tried, but finding a little privacy comes about as easily at her house as finding sacks of money dropped on the front porch. No matter how hard she tried, she couldn't find a time or place where her little brothers weren't trying to sneak in. And since her mom didn't really understand what Kresha was trying to do, she wasn't a whole lot of help. Kresha keeps hoping God understands.

In chapter 1 we discussed Jesus' habit of taking time to get away with God for long, private talks. *But—yikes!* you might be thinking. *He's Jesus, for heaven's sake. Everybody isn't like that. Aren't some people better at talking to God in a group? Maybe it's not easy for some people to talk to God alone. And what if the way their house is run makes it impossible for them to have quiet time even if they want to? Doesn't God know all that? Does he really expect everyone to practice this discipline?*

Yes, he does. But before you panic because you can totally relate to Reni or Suzy or Kresha or Zooey (and come on, how many of us are exactly like Lily!), remember that God wouldn't ask you to do something that's impossible. No matter who you are and what your home life is like, you can hang with him in a way that makes life so much better.

HOW IS THIS A God Thing?

Let's look at Reni's situation first. She has trouble turning off the noise in her head so she can concentrate on God. Life is busy, and it's hard to turn off its chatter in your brain. So how did Jesus do it?

When Jesus knew he had to wrestle with the Devil about something, he didn't try to do it in his usual surroundings. He knew he needed to be in a quiet place where he could be away from distractions. So he went into the wilderness (Matthew 4:1).

Now, that doesn't mean that Reni (or you, if you have Reni's same issue) have to head for the jungle or the desert or the mountaintop—as if you even *could!* It

does mean that it might be helpful for you to find a place for quiet time where you can get away from schoolbooks, the telephone, and the piano you need to practice. Reni finally settled into quiet time when she rediscovered the great climbing tree in the corner of the backyard, the one she always used to clamber up when she was a little kid. In good weather it makes a great getaway. There's nothing to remind her of all the other stuff she needs to do. When it's raining or cold, she heads for the back of her closet, where she has some pillows and a flashlight ready. The amazing thing is that sometimes she can now de-clutter her mind without having to be in one of her special places.

What about Suzy? If you're like her, you're anxious about "doing it right." Being all by yourself with God—and *realizing* you're all by yourself with God—can seem pretty scary. It's good to be so in awe of God that you want everything to be perfect. God loves the honor and respect, but he doesn't want you to be cowering in the corner or trying to make a good impression on him. Jesus had a plain and simple solution. Here's what Jesus said to do:

> When you pray, go into your room, close the door and pray to your Father, who is unseen.
> Matthew 6:6

So if you're like Suzy, find your quiet space, sit back, close your eyes, and just say to God everything you want to say, the same way you would to any trusted friend. The only difference is that God is much more than just a friend. He is the Ultimate Friend, the Friend of All Friends, the Friend who will keep all your secrets and put solutions into your head and make you feel glad all over.

But for Zooey that's easier said than done. If you're like Zooey, you need a little more structure. You could babble on for days, but you wouldn't hear what God had to say. It is, after all, a two-way conversation!

Now, Jesus wasn't one for giving specific instructions for your quiet time with God, but he did provide an outline, which has become known as the Lord's Prayer (Mathew 6:9–13).

We're not saying you should just pray the Lord's Prayer and you're good to go! But when you're alone with God and don't know where to start, use it as a guide for your conversation, like this:

"Our Father in heaven, hallowed be your name." Start by telling God how awesome he is and where and when you saw him doing his awesome thing today or yesterday. Get into the habit of looking for God things so you can report back to him.

"Your kingdom come, your will be done on earth as it is in heaven." Turn everything over to him, because he is, after all, in charge. Tell him about all the stuff that's bugging you, and the things that are hurting people you know. Give each of your concerns to him and ask him to help things work out his way. Ask him to set up kingdom-residence right inside you.

"Give us today our daily bread." Ask God for the things you really need, and remember that nothing is too small. Talk each item through with him, because you may find out that you don't really *need* a particular thing after all. But you always need his guidance and strength. So ask for that in every little detail of your life. Oh, and don't overlook that word *us.* If you know other people's needs, talk to God about those too.

"Forgive us our debts, as we also have forgiven our debtors." This is where you tell God all about the rotten, lousy stuff you've thought and said and done, and the good, sensitive things you either meant to do and didn't, or failed to even think of until now. Of course, God isn't so willing to forgive you and take all that stuff off your hands if you aren't willing to do it for the people who have done rotten, lousy stuff to you! This is a good place to talk to God about your hurt feelings and your anger and your grudges, and get those worked out. Give the whole enchilada to God. (There's more on this in chapter 5, so keep reading!)

"And lead us not into temptation, but deliver us from the evil one." Tell God about the tempting things, the evils around the corner, that you have to deal with, and ask for his protection. In fact, ask him to get that stuff right out of your life so you can concentrate more on the good things. And don't forget to ask him to let you see the little things you haven't noticed—like the way a new "friend" is using you, or the way you've been pulled into gossiping with the Girlz.

"Yours is the kingdom and the power and the glory forever." (This part isn't in the Bible but has been added by some churches. I don't think God minds at all!) Finish your conversation by telling God again that you know he's in charge and that you're willing to do whatever it takes to stay close to him.

Zooey, and *you,* may not realize it at first, but you've not only prayed but also done some important Bible study. We'll talk more later about reading the Bible, but this is a really good start.

Kresha, who can't seem to find a minute of peace and quiet in her life, has a problem similar to the one Jesus had—and the one you may have as well. Almost every time Jesus went off by himself to pray, people found him.

When Jesus learned his friend John the Baptist had died, "he withdrew by boat privately to a solitary place. Hearing of this, the crowds followed him on foot from the towns" (Matthew 14:13).

After Jesus had been teaching all day—and providing lunch for five thousand people—"he went up on a mountainside by himself to pray" (Matthew 14:23). But what happened? He returned to his disciples all glowing with God, even able to walk on water, and they freaked out on him. So much for peace and quiet.

Jesus tried getting up early in the morning—"while it was still dark, Jesus got up, left the house and went off to a solitary place, where he prayed." Who'd have thought that Simon and the others would find him at that hour? "Everyone is looking for you!" they said (Mark 1:35–37).

Kresha—and you if you and Kresha are two of a kind—can learn from the way Jesus dealt with his lack-of-privacy issue.

Jesus was very creative in finding places and times to get alone with God. You may not have access to boats and mountaintops, and getting up way before dawn might be out of the question, but the point is that Jesus simply used what was available to him and so can you. Is there some spot you can settle into during your day? A corner table at the school library during lunch for just ten minutes? The bench under a tree while you wait for your mom to pick you up? The laundry room after you finish folding the clothes? (Who's going to want to come in *there?*)

Jesus used the time he had, before people found him. He got down to the business of prayer right away, knowing that he would soon be discovered.

Jesus didn't scream at people when they interrupted him. He just accepted that his quiet time was over and got on with his day.

Jesus didn't look for big blocks of time but snatched up little moments whenever he could. "Crowds of people came to hear him and to be healed of their sicknesses," the gospel of Luke tells us. "But Jesus often withdrew to lonely places and prayed" (Luke 5:15–16). So instead of sitting enthroned on your bed for thirty minutes after school, you might have to take ten minutes in the bath in the morning, five minutes next to your favorite tree on the playground during recess, and fifteen minutes in the faraway laundry room while your mom is wrestling your little brothers into bed. It's actually a good way to learn to weave your relationship with God into your entire day.

CHECK Yourself OUT

Let's find out the best way for you to get some good quiet time alone with God. This quiz will help you discover what your special challenges are. Finish each statement by circling the letter of the ending that best fits you. If none of them are perfect for you, choose the one that's closest. Then read what your choice tells you.

Being Alone

If I suddenly found myself alone in my bedroom with the door closed:

A. I would love it!
B. I would be a little nervous at first, but I think I'd like it.
C. I would be freaked out and fling open the door!

If you circled *A*, this whole quiet-time thing is going to come very naturally to you. You're ready to find your time and space and go for it. Read on!

If you circled *B*, trust that you're going to learn to love quiet time, even if you're not quite sure about it right now. Give yourself a chance. Soften it with some low-key music you enjoy. Snuggle up with your cat or a stuffed animal. Make your time cozy and friendly. We'll tell you more about that as you read on.

If you circled *C*, you might be thinking that this is going to be tough—if not downright impossible! But don't despair. Just because it freaks you out a little to think of sitting around by yourself in silence doesn't mean you can't do it. And besides, who said anything about total silence? You can play music, talk out loud to God, or read your Bible aloud. It might even help to do your alone thing at a time when you know a friend is also doing hers. Start off with just ten minutes at first and give God your total attention. Then you can build up as quiet time becomes more comfortable. God would rather have a short session with you completely focused than a half hour of you wishing it would be over!

Finding the Right Place

If I could choose any place that exists in my life right now to hang out alone:

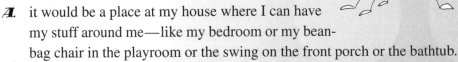

A. it would be a place at my house where I can have my stuff around me—like my bedroom or my bean-bag chair in the playroom or the swing on the front porch or the bathtub.

B. it would be a secret place close to the house that nobody else knows about—like that tree in the backyard or that old bench behind the garage.

C. it would be a place away from home where it's still safe to be by myself—like the guest bedroom at my after-school baby-sitter's house or the backseat of the van when we're waiting for my sister at her piano lesson or the next-door neighbor's screen porch where she lets me sit after I walk her dog.

If you circled *A*, your house is pretty quiet-time friendly and you like to be there. That makes it convenient, so you go, girl! Find your spot and snuggle in.

Just be sure you won't be interrupted and that your need for quiet isn't going to be a problem for everybody else in your house. If you decide to have your quiet time in a corner of the family room while your sister's entertaining her friends, it would be asking a lot to have them speak in sign language while you pray!

If you circled *B*, you really like "secret places." That can make your quiet time very sacred. Just be sure you aren't taking over anybody else's space—shoving your dad's tools out of the way to make yourself a place in the garage, for instance. And make sure your mom or dad knows where you are. Parents get a little frantic when their kids are missing in action!

If you circled *C*, you probably have a busy, away-from-home life and will need to carve out space wherever you can. It may not seem very special or sacred to you, but it *can* be. Is there a special pillow you can keep there? Can you pull out your special talking-to-God journal? It's your attitude that makes this time meaningful, so present yourself to God knowing he's going to provide what it takes for you to have some good time together. There are two of you in this, after all!

Choosing the Right Time

Looking at my Monday-through-Friday schedule:

A. I think I have at least thirty minutes a day to spend with God.
B. I think I probably have about ten to fifteen minutes to spend with God.
C. I don't think I have any time to spend with God, unless you count the two minutes while I'm falling asleep at night.

If you circled *A*, your schedule already has an opening for God. *Use* that time. Write it on your calendar if you keep one. Promise God and yourself that those thirty minutes (or maybe even more) belong to the two of you. That doesn't mean this is the only time you spend with God. All the spiritual disciplines are designed to bring you closer to God all the time. You just need this very centered time to help get you to that place.

If you circled *B*, you have a place to start at least. That ten to fifteen minutes you found? *Use* that time to be very focused on God. Promise God and yourself that those minutes are sacred, and you won't spend them on anything else. It's a pretty safe bet that as you really get into it, that time is going to stretch to twenty or thirty minutes, and you're going to wonder where the extra time came from!

If you circled ℭ, you don't have a lot of down time in your life, do you? That's hectic for anybody, let alone an eight- to twelve-year-old girl. Really look at all the things you're doing during the day. Write them all down if you have to. What are you doing that (1) you don't really have to do, and (2) you don't especially enjoy? That does *not* include going to school and doing homework and baby-sitting your little sister. But it might include the gymnastics class you've been taking since you were four, which you're now trying to squeeze in between soccer practice and dance class. Or it might point you to the hour you spend watching reruns on TV after school. Could you cut that to thirty minutes and devote the other thirty to God? Think about it. Pray about it. Your God time will show up for you.

Communicating with God

If I had a time and a place for quiet time:

A. I would choose to jot down my prayers in my journal, and write about what I'm learning from the Bible, and doodle while I'm listening for God's whisper.

B. I would choose to draw pictures of what I want to say to God and then draw designs of what I'm thinking after I pray and maybe do some sketches of people in the Bible, or sing to God and make up songs about him and put Bible verses to music, or play with clay the whole time I'm talking to God and listening.

C. I would choose to talk to God out loud while I'm swinging on my special swing at the playground, or jumping on our backyard trampoline before the other kids get home from school, or standing on my head in my bedroom.

If you circled *A*, writing is a great way for you to communicate with God, especially at first. You might want to keep your talking-to-God journal separate from any other journal or diary you keep. Or maybe not—maybe it all ties together. Having a special pen or a collection of pens makes the time different from any other time (like homework time!). Decorating your journal or notebook with your favorite Bible verses is cool to do. Write to your little heart's content, making sure that you're pausing to listen for God—perhaps closing your eyes so you can better hear and see what God is telling you. Those surprise thoughts just could be his whisper.

If you circled *B*, try using your creative gift in your quiet time. (If you're attracted to this approach but don't think you *have* a creative gift, you definitely need to get a copy of *The Creativity Book* right away!) Perhaps you could have special tools in your quiet space, like a sketch-book and colored pencils or your little keyboard, so when God's inspiration strikes, you're ready. Just be sure you're continually focusing on God, so you don't get so caught up in the painting or the song or the clay figure that you forget why you're doing it! God gave you the gift. He's waiting for you to use it to draw closer to him.

If you circled ℭ, you're so active that it's hard for you to sit still, so don't force yourself to. Use that energy and let it flow right to God as you dance while you're praying or swing higher and higher while you're listening. It's a little hard to read the Bible while you're standing on your head, but there are always tapes, or you can act out what you're reading, or you can walk around while reading it out loud. And who knows? You may get so involved, you'll find yourself sitting down and quietly soaking it in. Stranger things have happened!

Reading the Bible

If I'm supposed to read and study the Bible during quiet time:

𝔄. I think I'll enjoy that. I like reading the Bible.
𝔅. I think I'll have to get somebody to help me, because when I read the Bible, I don't always understand it.
ℭ. I think I'll skip that. It sounds like a lot of work.

If you circled 𝔄, you've probably already been taught how to read and study the Bible, and chances are, you have a Bible you can really understand and maybe a guide book to help you. You're set. Your next step is to find the parts of the Bible that talk about things you might be struggling with in your life right now. If your Bible doesn't have an index of topics (like "jealousy," "anger," "parents," "siblings," that kind of thing), ask an adult who really seems to live out the Bible's teachings to help you find what you need. Of course, if you would rather follow the devotions in a book or in what you bring home from Sunday school, that's perfectly fine. Either way you have so many cool discoveries ahead of you.

If you circled 𝔅, you're on the right track. You definitely don't want to stumble through a bunch of verses that make no sense to you and say, "Okay, did that. Next?" So first of all, get yourself a Bible that's easy for someone your age to understand. *The NIV Young Women of Faith Bible,* for example, was specially designed for girls eight to twelve years old. If such a purchase isn't in the family budget right now, maybe you can borrow one from your church or from a friend. Don't see any options? Start praying. If you want to read the Bible, you *know* God's going to make sure you get one! Most young people's Bibles have explanations and guides built right into them, and there are also devotional books like Susie Shellenberger's *Dear Diary: A Girl's Book of Devotions.* Don't think you're dumb just because you can't always understand the Bible all by yourself. Are you kidding? There are thousands of books out there to help *adults* get the most out of their Bible reading!

If you circled ℂ, you aren't alone. A lot of grown-ups have that same issue. But don't skip it. The Bible is one of the most important ways through which God speaks to us. The people who wrote the books of the Bible were divinely inspired when they wrote them—and you are divinely inspired when you read them. So let's get you started. Try reading stories from a Bible storybook—one that's not too young for you, of course. Get to know the characters and find out how they got close to God so they could live God-led lives. Know any kids who really seem to get into the Bible? Ask them about their favorite verses and take a look at those in a Bible, hopefully one put together for kids your age (like *The NIV Young Women of Faith Bible* we talked about in 𝔹 above). Pretty soon you'll need to read 𝔹, and then 𝔸! Just take it slowly at first. Nibble and snack on verses until you really understand them. Watch how they work during the day. God is going to love seeing you do that.

Just Do It

Are you ready to give this a go? None of the following steps are going to be a surprise to you, because we've talked about all of them already. This is just a down-to-the-bare-bones way to lay it all out so you won't be confused. As you complete the steps, think about what you've learned about quiet time from the "How Is This a God Thing?" section and what you've discovered about yourself in the "Check Yourself Out" department. You're about to put together a custom-designed quiet-time plan for yourself. Hey, girl! It's all about you and God.

Step 1.

Pray. Start right now, asking God to guide you in making this happen. Do it every day. Do it whenever it comes into your mind. Ask someone else to pray for you, too. After all, this is important stuff.

Step 2.

Let your parents know you're going to start having quiet time every day, and try to get their support. If they know what you're up to, they might offer to help by keeping younger siblings at bay, coming up with an appropriate Bible or some Bible guides, or remembering not to interrupt you between 7:00 and 7:30 when you have your door closed. If they're open to it, ask them to pray too.

Step 3.

Decide on your time and write it here: _____. Remember to take a good look at your schedule. Give up some little thing if you need to. Be realistic. Don't expect yourself to get out of bed at 5:30 in the morning (unless you're really an early bird), or plan to stay up later than your bedtime if you know that isn't going to fly with your folks.

Step 4.

Choose your quiet-time place and write it here: _____. If it's someplace other than your room, don't commandeer the space until you've checked it out with the right people. If you've selected someplace outside, have a backup plan in case of bad weather.

Step 5.

Do some little thing to make your space special if it isn't already. Comfortable pillows, your favorite God-reminder such as a cross or a fish (just exactly what are those wonderful fish called, anyway?), any tools you might want to use such as art supplies. Those small touches can help you focus right away. Of course, you can have quiet time with nothing but a Bible, and that's fine, too—whatever works for you and God.

Step 6.

Get yourself a Bible you can really understand. If you think a devotional guide would help, get one of those too. Make sure those items are right at your fingertips when quiet time starts, so you don't have to spend five minutes running around yelling, "Has anybody seen my Bible?"

Step 7.

Are you still praying? If you are, then quiet time has already started, right inside you.

Step 8.

Now let it happen. Show up at the appointed time and place and present yourself to God. Your own time with God will unfold in a sacred way. The disciplines you'll want to practice to help you grow spiritually should include the following:

- devoting yourself completely to God right at the beginning
- praying
- reading and studying the Bible in a way that helps you in your life right now
- listening—waiting for God to whisper his way into your thoughts and to stir up good, strong feelings in you

Warning: If you do all these things, God is going to ask you to change some things about yourself. Be ready to make those changes, or quiet time will be just something you add to your schedule.

Girlz WANT TO KNOW

✿ *LILY: What do you mean God's going to ask me to change? That sounds kind of scary to me! Is he going to ask me to do something weird? My parents aren't going to like that.*

Lily, Lily! Relax, girl! Who said anything about "weird"? God doesn't want us to be weird. He wants us to be our true selves. The kinds of changes he's going to ask for are going to take you closer to that "real you" he created you to be. We're talking about things like being more honest, being more patient, listening to people more—including the left-out kids—instead of always being the one talking. Get the idea? And when God puts it into your mind that you need to make a change, you won't be able to put up with yourself until you do it.

Here's what that might look like. Let's say you've been praying for some kids at school who always get left out of stuff. Maybe Ashley and her gang make fun of them all the time. You really feel sorry for them, so you've been praying about their predicament. You've been reading in the Bible about how Jesus chose those kinds of people to hang out with and even invited some of them to be his disciples.

More and more it's coming into your mind that you can't just sit back and pray for those kids. And you can't just "be nice to them." God is asking you—through your own nagging thoughts—to actually include them. It isn't going to be easy. The other Girlz might not want the girl who always picks her nose sitting at your table during lunch. And you're really going to be letting yourself in for some major harassment from Ashley and her crew. But God's asking you to make a change—we warned you about that—and you've got to do it. But don't worry, Lily. He's going to help you.

✿ *RENI: I'm already in a Bible-study class at church. Do I have to study it more on my own—or is that enough?*

Reni, the truth is that you can almost never get enough of what the Bible has to teach you. And the Bible study you're involved in at church is to help you *learn about* the teachings of Jesus and the history of God's relationship with his people. The Bible study you're doing at home is to help you *apply* God's Word to things that are happening to you personally.

For example, let's say the other kids in the orchestra are saying you think you're always the best in the violin section, things like that. And let's say in your quiet time with God, you discover that you really are getting kind of puffed up and proud about your playing. So with some help from your mom, who really knows her Bible, you use some of your quiet time with God to read about gifts and talents and how you're supposed to use them.

Let's say she also helps you find some sections that deal with humility. As you study them and try to picture Jesus talking straight to you, you begin to see ways to live out God's Word. You give more compliments to the other violinists. You don't brag about how you made All-City and All-State Orchestras. You apply what you learn directly to your life. See how that works?

✿ *KRESHA: When I pray, I imagine Jesus sitting there with me. Maybe we're sharing an order of fries. I can close my eyes and know how his voice sounds to me. Is that okay?*

It's absolutely okay! Some of the finest Christians in history have used a vision of the Lord to focus their prayers. In fact, you can probably ask any believer what he or she thinks God looks like, and you'll get an answer. Some of us are very visual people—we learn best by seeing. You're obviously one of those, and it was God who made you that way. So why not use that particular gift to draw nearer to him?

The only danger is in getting so attached to God's image that you miss something that he's trying to share with you about himself—like the fact that he's everywhere at all times or that his Holy Spirit fills you or that he works in unseen ways. Just don't miss out on the mystery, and you'll be fine. Use that wonderful imagination of yours (but please don't put him in plaid Bermuda shorts and black knee socks—that isn't a good look for anybody!).

✿ *ZOOEY: I know you said there's no right or wrong way to pray, but sometimes I feel like I'm asking for dumb things—you know, like "God, please help me know the answers on this test, and I promise next time I'll really study." And our pastor said in a sermon once that some things are just God's will. So what if what I'm asking for isn't God's will?*

First of all, Zooey, God knows you're just learning about prayer. If you're talking to him, he's listening. Did you think he might say, "Zooey, honey, come back and talk to me when you've learned how to do it right"? Uh, no. Now, if you want your prayers to be answered, you might follow these guidelines:

- God isn't going to do for you what you could have done for yourself but just plain didn't—like study for that test. God is in every detail of our lives, but part of that is that he expects us to take care of business.
- There are some things that we already know are God's will. God wants every person to become the self he created. And God wants his people to take care of their bodies and refuse to destroy them with alcohol and drugs and reckless driving and things like that. You get the idea? So you can certainly pray that your cousin will stop taking drugs or that the girl in school who is always yelling at you will get some help for her anger problem.
- When you're confused about what to do about a situation, you can pray about it by just giving it to God and saying, "Please help me work this out."
- Ask for a miracle if you feel you need to. Why shouldn't you expect God to do the things only God can do?
- God will always answer. Just remember that sometimes he says no. And if he does say no, that's the right answer.

Talking to God About It

Should we talk to God about how we're going to talk to him? Of course! We need to talk to him about everything! Let's do something a little different this time, though. Make the very first time you meet God in your quiet time and space very special. This is big stuff, so you might want to do some of the following:

- Dress just for God. That might mean wearing the best outfit you have or dressing as simply as you can. Maybe you have the urge to wear all white or to be plain and subdued.
- Give your space a sacred touch. You might have a cross you'd like to display or maybe a special cross-stitch of a Bible verse that your grandmother made for you. What about some pretty flowers?
- Bring a self-offering to God. Is your gift singing? If so, why not sing God a praise song or a hymn you love? Do you write poetry, draw pictures, collect shells, do amazing French braids? Share your gift with God at this first quiet time.

• Start a simple sacred ritual. With Mom's permission, light a candle, and as you put it out at the end of quiet time, ask Jesus to continue to be the Light that shines in you. Or draw a picture of something that's meaningful for you and reminds you of God. Or learn a Bible verse that you whisper each time you begin your quiet time with God. Rituals, like Holy Communion or prayers before a meal, have always helped God's people focus on his love.

• Do whatever you think of that will help you present your most real, reverent self to God. He deserves it, doesn't he?

If I could have quiet time anywhere, it would be . . .

Your Life –
It's Such a Simple Thing

Where your treasure is, there your heart will be also.
Matthew 6:21

You may be thinking to yourself, *My life? Simple? You've got to be kidding!*

For openers, you have school, which is far from simple—demanding teachers, teasing kids, tons of work, endless rules. And that's just the good stuff, right? Then there's your home life—chores to do, homework to finish, siblings to deal with, the phone to negotiate over. Plus you want to do fun stuff, like pursue hobbies, work on creative projects, hang out with friends, and schedule some down time.

"How," you may ask, "can my life possibly be *simple?*"

It would help to start with what we mean by a more simple life. Here's what it looks like:

- You are free from having to keep up with what everybody else owns or does or says is cool.
- You can be exactly who you are right now—no trying or pretending to be who people seem to expect you to be.
- You're honest.
- You aren't anxious about being first, the best, or the fastest.
- You don't have a bunch of stuff you don't really need—and may not really want.
- You enjoy what you do have.
- You're generous with your time, your stuff, and yourself.
- You trust God for everything.

Just reading that kind of makes you want to give a big sigh, doesn't it? Wouldn't it be wonderful to truly feel that way? You can if you bring simplicity into your life—inside and out.

In this chapter we're going to show you how to make your life simpler for God. Let's talk about how the spiritual discipline of simplicity will bring you closer to him.

HOW IS THIS A God Thing?

It's no accident that Jesus taught *and* lived a simple life. He knew the Scriptures and believed in the tenth commandment: "You shall not covet your neighbor's house. You shall not covet your neighbor's wife, or his manservant or maidservant, his ox or donkey, or anything that belongs to your neighbor" (Exodus 20:17). That "anything" included an endless list of covetable things like the following:

- how easy school is for your sister
- how pretty your best friend is
- how popular the new girl in your class is
- how easy it is for some of the girls in your class to make friends
- the way one particular kid always gets picked to read or pass stuff out or run errands for the teacher
- the clothes the girl next door wears
- the attention your brother gets because he's good in sports

You could probably make up your own list, and if you're really honest, it might be long enough to wrap you up like a mummy. Jesus would say to you, as he did to the people he taught, that you can't really live the life he's planned for you if you're so busy wishing you had all the things everybody else has.

Jesus said, "No one can serve two masters" (Matthew 6:24), meaning either God is in charge of your life or all the things you're so worried about are in charge of your life. "You cannot serve both God and Money." You either look to God to show you how to live or you let what everybody else has or is doing show you how to live.

So what does that look like in real life?

Lily wants to be accepted at school, just as everyone else does. She feels like a misfit a lot of the time, and sometimes she gets really sick of it. She has two choices:

1. She can check out the way Ashley and her friends behave, what they wear, how they talk, and then copy that exactly. It might mean saying some words her parents don't like her to say, so she sounds cool. It would also involve slipping into the restroom when she gets to school to plaster on some makeup, even though her mom has told her no makeup until she's older. It would definitely require her to put other kids down, since that's pretty much what Ashley and her crew talk about all the time. The popular kids would probably accept Lily, but she'd have to keep working at it all the time.

2. She can go to God in her quiet time and ask—every day until it comes to her—"Who do *you* want me to be? Who am I, really?" It will mean being completely honest with herself. It will involve figuring out that she doesn't really like short vinyl skirts and tops that expose her entire midriff right down to her belly button. It will definitely require her to accept exactly who she is right now and focus on how she's going to be even more real tomorrow. Lily will be accepted—by God, by herself, and by anyone else who appreciates a person who is always comfortable with who she is and doesn't have to worry about what people are going to think of her. After a while she won't feel as though it's work.

It doesn't take a college degree to see the difference:

- Coveting someone else's life can lead to talking in a way you shouldn't, but learning to live your own life makes your speech honest and clean.
- Coveting someone else's life can lead to disobeying your parents, but learning to live your own life brings you closer to the people you love and respect.
- Coveting someone else's life can lead to treating other people badly, but learning to live your own life lets you do what's right without having to worry about what someone thinks about you.

Jesus definitely saw the difference, and he was always telling the people (and us) not to be so hung up on possessions and money and achievements. Remember when Jesus told the rich young ruler to get rid of everything he owned if he really wanted to be in God's kingdom? Do you recall Jesus telling the disciples that whatever was important to them was going to determine all their decisions? It was going to decide for them how much they really loved God (Matthew 19:16–30).

Now, before you get nervous and think we're going to tell you to toss all your CDs and stuffed animals in the trash—relax. God wants us to have all that we need. He also wants us to enjoy what we have. Those two words, *need* and *enjoy,* can help you know what God wants you to have—and what crowds your life and keeps it from being simple.

- Do you *need* six pairs of new jeans?
- Do you really *enjoy* participating in a different sport or activity every day after school?
- Do you *need* that jacket that costs more than the rest of your wardrobe put together?
- Do you really *enjoy* freaking out over every test and school project because you want to be perfect?

If you have trouble answering those questions, or the ones you come up with yourself, all you have to do is go to God—just the way you learned to in chapter 2—and begin to discover the answers. It's that simple.

 ## CHECK Yourself OUT

Let's find out just how simple—or not so simple—your life is right now. Remember, this quiz is not designed to point out how "badly" you're doing! It's supposed to give you a fun peek at some things you might not have noticed.

Finish each of the following statements by circling the letter of the ending that best fits you. If you don't find a perfect fit, get as close as you can.

Keeping Up with the Crowd

If everybody—meaning everybody who's anybody—was carrying one of those tiny little purses with a long shoulder strap that cost $9.99:

   A. I would try to get my mom to buy me one in every color so I'd have them to match all my outfits.

   B. I would use my allowance to get one, just so I wouldn't feel like a loser.

   C. I wouldn't buy one. You can't even fit your lunch money in there!

Life's Necessities

If somebody took away something that I have to have every day (like television, chocolate, soda, video games, hour-long phone conversations, and email):

A. I would flip out completely. Seriously, I'd either cry or sneak around so I could have it. I might even lie or steal.

B. I would try to bargain for just a little of it. I don't think I could go cold turkey.

C. I wouldn't care. I can't even think of anything like that in my life, so I don't think I have to worry about it.

Giving Things Away

If I looked around my room, thinking maybe I could give some of my stuff away:

A. I would be a little freaked out. I can't think of anything I'd want to part with.

B. I'd be able to come up with a couple of things at least. I might even get into it once I got started.

C. I'd think that was a cool idea and I'd get right on it.

New Gadgets

If somebody came out with a minicomputer—with sparkles on it—that would keep track of all my friends' phone numbers and birthdays and favorite colors and all that:

A. I would have to have it. Really—I *need* that.

B. I'd like to see one, but I don't know if I'd actually ask my dad to buy me one.

C. I wouldn't even think about getting one. Who needs it? I already have a cool address book that I made myself.

Shopping Sprees

When I go shopping with my mom or my friends:

A. I have to buy something or it isn't any fun.

B. I like to look at stuff, see what's out there, dream about what it would be like to have all the things I like.

C. I think about how I'd rather be at the zoo or the park or the lake or something. I'm not a big shopper.

Being Honest

When my friends and I are talking:

A. I sometimes exaggerate a little, just so everybody will like my story more. That's okay, isn't it?

B. I'm always afraid somebody will think what I'm saying is stupid or weird or something, so I'm really careful about what I say.

C. I just say whatever's true. What else am I supposed to do?

Let's find out what your answers could mean.

If you circled mostly **A**s, take a close look at your life. Do you really go nuts over new fads and trends? Are you practically addicted to something like TV or videos or Peanut M&Ms? Is your room piled with stuff—stuff you couldn't bear to part with even though you never use half of it? Are you always wanting more? Is even your speech cluttered up with things that aren't exactly true, though they sure make you sound good? If the answer to those questions is yes, that doesn't mean you're a gross, disgusting person! It means you *really* need this chapter. It means you have the chance to make some big changes in your life that are going to make it so much happier. Trust us—you have some exciting things ahead of you.

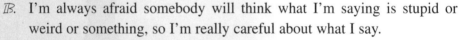

If you circled mostly *B*s, you probably want to live a simpler life than the one you're living, but sometimes it's hard for you. Maybe you like that feeling of being like the other kids a *lot*. Maybe you feel you don't have a whole bunch of stuff, so you would just as soon not give any of it away. Maybe it hadn't occurred to you to de-clutter your life—but you kind of like the idea. If that sounds like you at all, you are *so* ready for this chapter. We're going to show you how to do what you're secretly longing to do—and get some real God things in the bargain.

If you circled mostly *C*s, you're already on the road to a simpler life. Fads and trends and new gadgets aren't important to you. Having things is fine but you're not that attached to them. You're going to drink in this chapter like a chocolate milkshake (or the flavor of your choice!). When you finish, you're going to be able to enjoy what comes naturally to you. You and God are going to be so much closer than ever.

Just Do It

So how do you practice the spiritual discipline of simplicity?

There are two paths you have to take to simplicity, actually. One is the *inside* path to simplicity. The other is the *outside* path.

You need to take the inside path first, or the outside path will just be a bunch of rules and activities that don't mean anything—and will clutter up your life even more!

So let's go with that inside path now. There's only one thing you have to do: *"seek first [God's] kingdom and his righteousness"* (Matthew 6:33).

Piece of cake, right? Put God first and everything else will be simple.

Uh-huh, and how exactly do you *do* that?

You don't *do* anything. That's the whole point. It looks like this:

Simplicity Activity 1

Go to your quiet-time place. (Don't have it yet? Choose one just for now, someplace where you won't be interrupted for at least ten minutes.) Close your eyes. Get very quiet. Imagine God there with you (because of course he is!). Be as real as you can be. Chase out any excuses and cover-ups or mean thoughts, like jealousy and hatred and resentment. Even shoo out ideas that *you* want to give God, like prayers for people and ways you want to be amazing. Basically, get down to nothing before God.

It could take a while—maybe ten or fifteen minutes—before you get the hang of making room for God's voice. Then simply say, out loud if you're comfortable, "God, you come first with me. Please tell me how that's supposed to look in my life." Obviously, one little session with God isn't going to cover you forever! You'll want to include this activity in your quiet time every day. Then the outward path you take will lead you where it's supposed to—right to God.

Simplicity Activity 2

Only when you get it straight inside you that God comes first in your life, no matter what, will the simplicity steps make any sense or do any good. Warning: Don't just take these steps and think you're good to go. If you aren't doing them to make more room for God, don't do them at all. Otherwise you're a lot like the Pharisees Jesus was always yelling at, telling them they were all show. You don't want to go there. With that in mind, take these steps to simplify your life:

Step 1.

During a typical day in your life, when you're doing your normal thing, pay attention to anything that you just have to have or do. Without it you'll feel anxious. Maybe you go straight to the computer after school and play video games until your mom makes you shut it off. Or perhaps you talk on the phone every chance you get, pushing the limit until your dad threatens to ground you. It might be soda that consumes your thoughts until you get your hands on one—five or six times a day. Could it be television? Chocolate? Even reading? We're not talking about things that truly make you happy, like your cozy bedroom or time spent with your best friend. These "addictions" we're asking you to look for are things that keep you from other things that are healthy, including quiet time with God.

If you identify an "addiction"—and not everybody will—don't feel like a drug addict who has to rush to rehab! This is a pretty simple thing to fix. Just substitute something good, something healthy, that will bring you closer to God.

- When you get home from school, go chat with your mom and tell her about your day, instead of running for the computer games.
- Write a letter to somebody you haven't seen in a long time, instead of picking up the phone to talk to the friend you just spent six hours with at school.
- Ask your mom to buy juice instead of sodas, and ask yourself if you really want something sweet to drink. Maybe you're just thirsty for water. Or maybe you're just bored. If boredom is the culprit, do something that truly delights you.
- Instead of reaching for the TV remote, go to your quiet place and relax with God. Take that glass of juice or water with you if you want!

Step 2.

Go through the stuff you own—things you've bought or your folks have bought for you or you've received as gifts. Ask yourself some questions about each item or group of items:

- Have I used it in the last six months?
- Would it really make me unhappy if I didn't have it?
- Does it delight me?
- Do I have it and/or use it because it expresses who I really am, rather than impresses people or makes me feel like I belong in a group?
- Do I even remember why I absolutely had to have it in the first place?
- Does it bring back happy memories or make me think good thoughts— God thoughts?

If you answered no to any of those questions about an item, you might consider getting rid of it.

Maybe it's the twenty-five stuffed animals you barely look at anymore. Could you keep the five that have special memories for you and give the rest to your little sister or to a child who doesn't have any toys?

Maybe it's the little ceramic gymnastics figures on your shelf that used to help you daydream about being in the Olympics—only you haven't taken gymnastics for three years and you're now dreaming about playing professional women's basketball someday. Could those go into a yard sale or church tag sale?

Maybe it's the black belt with the silver studs on it that you had to have because everyone is wearing one, only it's really uncomfortable on you. Could you give it to the girl in your class who says she wishes she had one?

Get yourself two garbage bags. In one put the things you want to give away—either to somebody in particular or to the church yard sale or some other charity. In the other put the things you want to throw away—like those hundreds of old school papers, the insect collection you'd forgotten about, and all those old magazines that are gathering dust under your bed.

Before you head for the garbage can or the nearest charity, check with your mom and dad. That dresser scarf you're pitching might have been made by Great-Aunt Gussie—or your mom might want to keep a couple of your school papers (because moms do things like that). Then go for it. And enjoy all the space in your room!

Step 3.

Challenge yourself to see how many things you can enjoy without owning them.

- Does a friend have something you've been secretly wishing she'd get sick of and miraculously give to you? A ring? The coolest CD player on the planet? Tickets to see dc Talk in person? Challenge yourself to compliment her on it without saying you'd love to trade places with her—and be delighted that she has it.

- When you go shopping, do you find yourself begging for half the stuff you see or longing for one item until that's all you can think about? Challenge yourself to admire what you want as if you were in a museum or an art gallery. Enjoy the smell, the feel, the colors, and the possibilities. Then go on to the next thing. Turn a shopping trip into a sightseeing tour!

- Do you spend a lot of your free time going shopping or looking at catalogs or tuning in to a home-shopping network on TV? Challenge yourself to look at something else—go to a museum, an art gallery, a park, or even your own backyard. Look at books with gorgeous pictures. Lie on your back and look at the clouds. Observe your dog as he patrols the yard. Delight in the beautiful things around you.

Step 4.

Count your blessings. Take a look at what you now still have or can simply enjoy. Thank God for all that—in your quiet time and every time you think of it. There are things you can do to feel those blessings right down in your soul:

- Organize your stuff. Put like things together on shelves. Put books in order in the bookcase in a way that makes sense to you. Make clothes in your closet easy to find by putting pants together, blouses together, skirts together, dresses together. Straighten up the stuff in your drawers. Put art supplies in plastic bins if you have them. Make a special place for everything. As you handle each item, delight in it. God likes that.

• Organize your time. We talk about that a lot in *The Blurry Rules Book*. Until you can get your hands on a copy, simply look for things you do that waste time rather than just relax you. Make sure you have a balance of fun, healthy activities, quiet time with God, and down time in the hours when you aren't sleeping or going to school. Be sure you aren't too busy or have too much time on your hands. Time is a gift from God that you need to take care of. Streamlining your schedule simplifies your life.

• Take care of what you have. When you take your clothes off, stop throwing them around until you can't see the floor. Don't turn down the corners of pages in your books. Dust your collections. Train yourself not to put your feet on the wall when you're talking on the phone. What you have is a blessing to you. Respect that.

• Pay attention to *all* the things God has created. On your way to and from school really look at the trees, the birds, and the clouds. Challenge yourself to see one thing every day that you haven't noticed before. Use all your senses to check out God's creation wherever you go. Smell a puppy's breath. Run sand through your fingers. Listen to a baby's laughter. Roll a blackberry around in your mouth before you squish it with your teeth. Hold an autumn leaf up to the light and inspect its colors. It's such a simple thing to do—and it adds so much richness to your life with God.

Step 5.

Simplify the way you talk. That doesn't mean to start using only one-syllable words! Try these ideas to make your speech more of a God thing:

- Be as honest as you can all the time. It doesn't matter if someone gets mad at you. It doesn't matter if people think you're way different from them. It doesn't matter if you don't come off as cool as you'd like. What matters is that you're honest.

   The problem with exaggerating or covering up your mistakes or telling little white lies to make things go more smoothly is that after a while it's hard to remember what really is the truth. And if people find out you're not completely honest, they may not trust you when you *do* tell the truth.

   If you have trouble being honest, that's something you're going to want to talk about with God in your quiet time.

- Be true to your word. If you say you're going to do something, do it—whether it's taking out the trash or praying for your friend's grandmother. That means you need to be really careful about what you promise to do in the first place!

- Listen to other people as much as you can. Have you ever had a friend who always seemed to be thinking of the next thing she was going to say while you were talking? Try not to do that. Really hear what people are saying. Encourage them to talk by asking them questions. Show you're listening by nodding or reacting with "Oh!" or "Wow!" or even "You're kidding!"

- Clean up any talk that isn't pure. That doesn't mean drop all your slang! It means don't use dirty-sounding language—four-letter words, bathroom talk, that kind of thing. It means never using God's or Jesus' names in any way that isn't reverent to them. And it means dropping all put-down words—things like *geek, dummy, idiot, klutz, weirdo, loser,* and *stupid-head* (or any of your personal favorites!). Don't even call *yourself* those names. You've probably heard this saying from adults so much that it makes you roll your eyes, but it's true: If you can't say something nice, just don't say anything at all.

Step 6.

Always, always—oh, and did we say always?—put God first. If it's a choice between having your quiet time with God or lounging on the couch with a bag of popcorn, take the quiet time. If it's a toss-up between spending your allowance on one more Beanie Baby or buying your sister something to cheer her up, go with the sister gift. If you have to choose between a third dance class or a cool after- noon Bible study, think about which one God wants you to pick (and ask him!).

That's a lot to do. Don't try to do it all at once, and don't try to do it all by yourself. That's what quiet time is for—to talk to God about the things you can do to get closer to him, *and* to listen to the answers. Don't worry. They'll come, softly and gently, working their way into the way you talk and act and dress and spend your time. Enjoy the changes that are about to happen.

Girlz WANT TO KNOW

❀ *LILY: I've gone through my room three times, and I love everything I own! Seriously, I couldn't find anything I wanted to throw away or give to somebody else. Is that selfish? Am I, like, hoarding?*

It doesn't necessarily mean you're a selfish hoarder, Lily! In the first place, you're the kind of person who really does treasure what she has. It's very pos- sible that you just haven't accumulated unnecessary stuff. But here's one thing you can do to make sure—and to perhaps loosen up the hold you may have on things: Choose one thing that you're really attached to, something that isn't vital to your survival right now. You wouldn't, for instance, want to pick your school binder or your talking-to-God journal. But you could pick the CD you've been listening to over and over or the pinky ring you find yourself staring at several times a day. If it wasn't a gift and it isn't an heirloom or something, ask your mom or dad if you can give it to someone—preferably someone who would be overjoyed to get it, like Kresha.

Has one of your friends enjoyed that CD with you? Does the girl who sits next to you in class admire your ring—maybe because she doesn't seem to have any jewelry? In a very simple way, without a bunch of hoopla, give that attached-to-you possession away. At first you will feel a little sting of loss, but pay attention to what you feel after that. That's definitely a God thing (as long as you don't tell everyone how wonderful you were to give away your prized possession!).

✿ *ZOOEY: I'm just now starting to look decent in clothes, and my mom has bought me some really nice stuff. I like getting compliments on what I'm wearing. Is that bad? Do I have to give all my clothes away?*

No to both questions! There is nothing wrong with wanting to look your best, especially if you're dressing in styles that show who you are, rather than show that you can keep up with the latest trends. There's also nothing bad about enjoying compliments. Who doesn't? Where it gets tricky is if you're doing any of these things:

- Dressing *only* for the compliments. Choosing clothes just because you know someone is going to tell you that you're a knockout.
- Choosing an outfit because it's totally "in" and shows how hip you are, rather than because it expresses the real you.
- Getting so wrapped up in your wardrobe that you don't have quiet time or time for homework and chores or don't talk to your friends about things besides what you're wearing or what everybody else is wearing.

You definitely don't have to give all your clothes away! But what you might consider is this: The next time you and your mom go shopping and buy something new for you, go through your closet and your drawers and take out *(a)* some item you haven't worn in three months, *(b)* some item that no longer fits you, *(c)* some item you really don't like or feel comfortable in. Make a plan to give it away *before* you put your new stuff in its place. You'll be surprised at how generous you'll become.

🌸 *RENI: I'm having trouble with the clean-up-your-speech thing. I don't cuss or anything, but I tease my friends a lot—you know, just kidding around. Do I have to stop calling Lily a freak show when she gets a really out-there idea or just saying, "You're such a klutz, Kresha" when she trips for like the fortieth time?*

That's a tough one. On the one hand, you figure your friends know you're just kidding, so what's the harm? But on the other hand, Jesus was pretty specific when he said yes is yes and no is no and that should be it. Don't, in other words, say anything you don't really mean. If you don't really mean that Lily is a freak show, should you really say it? In fact, Lily may *say* she knows you're kidding, but how many times can she be called a freak show, even in jest, before she starts believing it?

But don't despair; you don't have to have a personality transplant! There are ways to keep that wonderful sense of humor of yours and purify your speech.

- Instead of picking "flaws" to tease about, comment playfully on the good stuff. "You have the most out-there ideas, Lily. I love it! What do you do, lie awake at night thinking of this stuff? Do you get them in the bathtub? Where do they come from?"
- Avoid name calling altogether. Nobody needs to have a label plastered on her, even if you mean it in fun. Instead pay a fun compliment. Not "You are such a freak show" but "You blow me away with your ideas, Lil'." Not "You're a klutz, Kresha" but "Graceful landing, Kresha. You never get embarrassed when you trip—that's so cool."
- Think about how sarcastic you are. Sarcasm can be really fun in the right place, but sometimes it means you're a little angry, a little unhappy with yourself. Do you tease Lily that way because you're tired of all her ideas and plans or because you're jealous that it's so easy for her to come up with

creative stuff? Talk to God about it, and then do whatever needs to be done to work it out. After all, simplifying your life is meant to bring you nearer to God *and* make things more peaceful and joyful in your daily life.

Talking to God About It

As we've been talking about all the stuff that can clutter up a girl's life, you've probably thought of some things that are keeping your own life from being as simple as it could be for God.

In the circle below write down everything that you *do* or *have* that has come to mind as we've talked about simplifying your life. Write any way you want, in any color you want, anywhere in the circle that strikes your fancy. Be honest. Don't leave out anything that really could go out of your life, especially anything that's separating you from what God wants for you. Go for it!

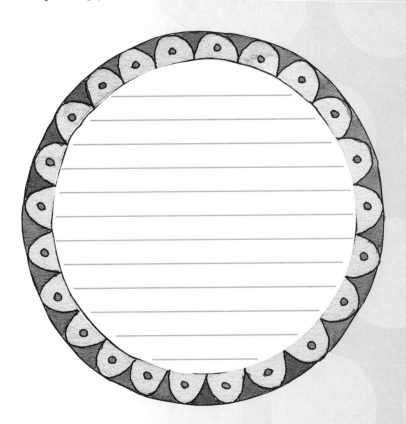

Now spend some quiet time with God, asking him to help you with every single one of those things. Ask him, "Do I need to get rid of it? Change it? Give it away? Ask somebody to help me get a handle on it?" If you ask, you'll get your answer. Keep listening. Keep watching. Keep obeying.

If I could only have ten things in my room, they would be . . .

It's Your Serve!

Jesus said, "Now that I, your Lord and Teacher, have washed your feet, you also should wash one another's feet."
John 13:14

Lily has what you might call a "noble spirit." She really loves the idea of doing big things to help people in ways that, as she puts it, "totally make a difference." Remember how she wanted to be a healer and cure everything from cancer to broken legs? And how she was determined to solve every problem that came to the "Answer Girl" box at the school newspaper? And what about the time she wanted to be a powerful advocate like Martin Luther King Jr. and ensure justice for all? Yeah, our Lily loves to serve—but as you know, her wonderful intentions can get way out of control.

Kresha has a heart the size of Montana. She'll give her lunch money to a kid who's lost his and go hungry herself. She's been known to give her coat to a homeless person and run on to school bare-armed in the snow. And heaven knows she'll drop everything—homework, supper, her next class—if one of the Girlz is in trouble and needs her help. Sometimes that's a good thing, and sometimes it gets her in a world of trouble.

Reni is so busy, it isn't always clear to her that somebody needs something from her. Of course once she knows, she'll try to do whatever is asked of her, but it just doesn't occur to her to look around and see where she can help out. She's certainly not a selfish person, but she's been called that on more than one occasion. It's a bummer.

Suzy loves to help out and do nice things for people, and now that she's going to church, she likes the idea of serving meals at the homeless shelter and other things the church does. But she's so shy, she doesn't sign up for them unless the other Girlz are going, too. And when she does join in, she's always afraid she isn't going to do something right and everyone will wish she'd stayed home. It pretty much takes the joy out of it for her.

Zooey would do anything for anybody if her mom would let her. Zooey's mother thinks it's wonderful that Zooey is so kindhearted, but she's afraid for her. What if she picks up germs at the homeless shelter? What if she spends a lot of time making cookies for a children's program at church and the kids don't appreciate it? What if she gets so tired from helping Kresha with her school project that she can't do a good job on her own? What if she's helping Suzy cope with her parents' divorce and she gets depressed? It's frustrating for Zooey, and she hopes people don't think she just doesn't care about others.

All the Girlz, just like you, want to be helpful. The idea of the spiritual discipline of service comes naturally to most people. It's one of the best parts of being human—stuff like opening doors for strangers, letting people go ahead of you in line when you can tell they're in a hurry, or even feeling the sting when one of your friends gets her feelings hurt.

So if wanting to help is automatic, why do you need to discipline yourself to do it? For a couple of reasons, really:

1. You need to be sure you have the right attitude. When you sign up to serve, is it all about you and how good you're going to feel and how impressed everybody's going to be? Or is it all about God giving you the nudge and you simply obeying because it's the thing to do?
2. You need to practice service with limits. Some things you attempt may be way over your head, which usually ends up causing even more problems than there were to begin with. Or you can take on too many projects and not do any of them well. It's also possible to focus so much on serving that you neglect your own needs.
3. You may have to make compromises on some of your service plans, since you're at an age when your parents are still deciding a lot of things for you. Just learning how to do that—without getting yourself grounded!—is an important part of your journey.

Yikes! If you're going to go through all that, this had *better* be a God thing, right? Let's take a look at that.

HOW IS THIS A God Thing?

Jesus wants us to copy the way he lived his life. He said so when he was washing his disciples' feet: "I have set you an example that you should do as I have done for you" (John 13:15). And it doesn't take more than a glimpse at the way he lived to see that what he wants us to copy is all about service.

- Jesus spent long hours—probably in the hot sun—teaching people, because he wanted so much for them to change their lives (Matthew 5:1–12, for example).
- Jesus stopped whatever he was doing to heal people who were suffering (Matthew 8:1–14).
- Jesus provided food for thousands of people because they'd been sitting for a whole day listening to him teach (Matthew 14:15–21).
- Jesus showed us exactly how to serve when he washed the feet of his disciples at the Last Supper (John 13:1–17).

And just in case we don't get it from the example he set, Jesus spells it out so we can't miss it: "Whoever wants to become great among you must be your servant, and whoever wants to be first must be your slave—just as the Son of Man did not come to be served, but to serve" (Matthew 20:26–28).

There's no getting around it. We're supposed to be servants, just like Jesus. Now let's figure out the best way to do that.

CHECK Yourself OUT

Picture the following scene, and then choose the reaction to it that sounds the most like you:

A girl who goes to your school—let's call her Katie—lost pretty much everything she had in a house fire. All she has left is what she was wearing and carrying at the time of the fire—her pajamas and an old stuffed rhinoceros, both now reeking of smoke. You and your friends don't know her well. As soon as you hear about it:

A. you feel bad for Katie and thank God it wasn't you or one of your close friends.

B. you think about giving Katie some of your clothes but decide not to because she might think they're stupid or wonder why you didn't buy her new ones.

C. you pack up most of your clothes, ready to give them to Katie right away.

D. you organize a huge fund-raiser to buy clothes for the entire family for the whole winter.

Before we talk about what your answer means, remember that it doesn't tell you whether your generosity puts Mother Teresa to shame or shows that you are the scum of the earth! As always, it's just a means to shed some light on the way you may be thinking right now, so you'll know what to talk to God about. We all have to know where we are before we can go where we need to go.

If you checked *A,* you have a kind heart. You care about what happens to people and you can even feel their pain, especially when those people are close to you. Your challenge is to learn to take action when someone needs help, rather than simply feeling bad for that person. Compassion, which is what you feel, is a wonderful thing, but you'll notice that Jesus didn't just look at the hungry, sick, miserable crowds and say,

"Wow—that's really sad. I feel awful for these folks." He went into the crowds and healed and fed and gave hope.

No, you aren't Jesus. You can't cure somebody's appendicitis with the touch of a hand. But you can do something. If you know someone has just had her appendix out, even if she isn't one of your best friends, you can take her a coloring book and a box of crayons so she won't get bored, or find out if you can take her homework to her, or just go visit and fill her in on what's been happening at school while she's been gone.

While you're there, she might even tell you about something else she needs. Think about times when you've been bummed out or sick or in trouble. Wouldn't it have been nice if someone had asked you, "What can I do for you?" Since we're supposed to love our neighbors as ourselves (Matthew 22:39), serving even in a small way is a God thing. This chapter will help you learn to practice that spiritual discipline.

If you checked *B,* you are kindhearted *and* you have good instincts about serving. You don't just feel bad for someone who's in need; you actually come up with ideas for what you can do to help. That's a God thing in you. But you tend to think that what you have to offer isn't good enough or you won't do it just right. This chapter is going to help you turn that thinking around, so you will know that any service that comes from an honest part of your soul is "good enough" and will be "done right." Think of it this way: If *your* house burned to the ground and *your* wardrobe was suddenly reduced to one pair of pajamas, would you rather have somebody else's slightly worn jeans and T-shirts—or nothing at all? Can you imagine yourself looking at the bearer of a pile of pants and dresses and tops and saying, "Let me look through these and see if there's anything I really want"?

What people usually appreciate most is that you thought of them and went out of your way to help. Now, if someone *does* throw your generous gift or offer of help back in your face, what's the worst that can happen? You'll feel bad. Period. Sure, you hate to feel bad, but when you talk to God about it in your quiet time, you'll figure out that God is really proud of you and that you have grown into a better person than you were before you tried. That kind of hurt goes away. The feeling that you should have helped and didn't stays around.

If you checked ℂ, you're one of those completely unselfish people who would give up everything they own if they knew someone was in need. You've been blessed with the gift of service, and that's definitely a God thing. This chapter is going to help you develop balance, so you don't leave yourself with nothing with which to help the next person who comes along—or help yourself when you need it.

Please don't think we're trying to pull you back from being generous! Don't let anyone tell you that you have to think of yourself first. But at this time in your life, you're just learning how to manage your time and your material possessions, and that means learning what to give away and how much of your time to spend filling other people's needs.

What if your mom had a friend whose child was in the hospital, and your mom spent all her time, 24/7, doing stuff for them—cooking meals for her friend's other kids, taking them to school and soccer practice, giving them baths and putting them to bed. And what if she were so busy that she didn't have time to do any of those things for *your* family? Not good!

It's the same for you. It would be wonderful if you gave Katie some clothes, but it wouldn't be wonderful to give away so many that you didn't have anything to wear yourself. It would be great for you to invite Katie over to play so she can get out of that motel room her family is now staying in, but it wouldn't be great if in that time you didn't get any of your homework or chores done.

In an extreme emergency, of course, you do whatever it takes to help. But in most situations, you can practice generosity and service without neglecting things you really need to do in your own life. Read this chapter carefully, practice, and, girl, you can make a real difference in other people's lives.

If you checked D, you love to go all out. There is nothing at all wrong with that. In fact, God loves it when your heart just overflows with ways to help other people. As you read this chapter and do the activities, you'll learn that to dream big is good and to pay attention to how God wants you to carry out those dreams is even better. If people didn't dream big in serving others, we wouldn't have penicillin or fire departments or Ronald McDonald Houses. But if the people who dreamed those dreams didn't have the resources to make them happen, their dreams would only be empty promises.

Suppose you announced that you were going to organize a major fundraiser for Katie and her family. Suppose you decided to hold an auction. But you didn't have time to call businesses to get them to donate items. And you didn't know anybody who could be the auctioneer. And you didn't have enough money to pay for the building in which to hold the auction. Katie and her family would be hoping for winter wardrobes for four, and you would feel that you'd let them down.

Wouldn't it be better to start small? Maybe you have a brand-new stereo you saved for and bought with your own money. You decide to have a drawing, and whoever has the winning ticket gets your stereo. You and your friends sell tickets, hold the drawing in your front yard, and raise fifty dollars. That could buy a winter coat and some other things for Katie. And who knows, maybe a local business learns about your raffle and decides to donate some items for another one or simply donates coats for the rest of the family.

In this chapter you'll learn how to start with what you can do and have faith that God will make it bigger in his own way. It's so much more fun to dream with God than by yourself anyway!

Just Do It

Before we plunge into service activities, there's one word we need to get to know really well, and that's *humility*. Take a look at the humility of God's Son:

Jesus hung out with people whom everybody else put down and wouldn't be seen with—like that woman at the well.

Jesus dug around in the mud to get the right stuff to cure somebody's sight.

Jesus washed his disciples' *feet!*

Jesus suffered whipping and spitting and nails in his hands—for us.

Service wasn't a glamour gig for Jesus. He was the Son of God—you can't get any higher in rank than that—yet he had to humble himself to do the job God sent him here to do: save lost, suffering, clueless people. He had to do it no matter what it took—standing out in the blistering sun for hours, picking wheat in a field to have something to eat, staying wherever he and his twelve buddies were invited in. And he had to do it without expecting anything in return. When he did get cheers and people wanted to make him king, he said no way. *That's* humility.

So when you're practicing the spiritual discipline of service, you need to do it with humility, just as Jesus did. That doesn't mean you should go down to the most dangerous part of town and start passing out sandwiches all by yourself (got that, Lily types?). It does mean that whatever service you do, you should:

- not expect it to make you popular.
- realize that some people will say you're nuts.
- be willing to do the jobs nobody else wants to do, which may involve getting dirty or being uncomfortable or watching other people raise walls while you sort nails.
- not expect any reward or praise.
- not bask in the limelight when people do praise you.

If any of these make you squirm and think, *Oh, I don't think I can do that,* write it here: _____.

In your next quiet time—or even right now—ask God to help you with this aspect of serving with humility. Then look out because sure enough, God is going to give you an opportunity to practice it!

Okay, now you're ready to go. It's hard to just up and do a service activity, because your opportunities to serve come in God's time. But chances are, God has something waiting for you, so let's start there.

Step 1.

For five days in a row, make a point to pray for God to make you aware of some service he wants you to perform for one of his children (kid or grown-up). In your journal write the ideas that come to you. Remember that the God thoughts can come to you anytime, not just while you're in your quiet space. Maybe you should have a notepad handy at all times! If this gives you trouble, think and pray about:

- already established church or community projects that you could join.
- anyone you know who's sick.
- a friend who's having a hard time.
- a teacher who seems stressed out.
- a brother or sister who's having trouble in school or in sports or in getting along with your mom and dad.
- a neighbor who seems lonely.
- a kid at school who is picked on or left out.
- anybody who has recently suffered a loss—for example, the death of a family member or a beloved pet.
- anyone who's going through a change—they're moving away, or their parents are divorcing or have lost their jobs.
- a person who wants to know God and can't quite get there.

Step 2.

If more than one idea comes to you, pray about your list. Think about the things we've already talked about in this chapter. One of those ideas will float to the top, and you'll know that's where you should start. Write your service idea here: _____. Pray some more until you really feel sure of it.

Step 3.

Now take a look at this "service checklist" and see how many of these criteria fit your idea. Put a star next to each one that does.

_____It comes from the kindness of your heart, not from some "have to" or "should" or "oughta."

_____It's an *action* you can take, not just a feeling you have.

_____It's something the person or people will probably welcome (rather than "I'm doing this for her own good").

_____You trust that this is a God thing, no matter how nervous you are about doing it.

_____You're prepared for somebody to say you're crazy or you're a goody-goody.

_____You will still be able to take care of your basic needs and responsibilities, like eating lunch and getting your schoolwork done.

_____It's possible and realistic for you to do this. You haven't planned a bigger task than you can possibly accomplish.

If you've put a star next to at least five of these, you're good to go. Take a look at the ones you didn't star and pray about those. Do what you have to do to get a star there. God is ready to help you, so take them to quiet time and pray about them whenever they come to mind during the day.

Step 4.

Chat with your mom or dad about what you're planning to do, especially if it involves giving something away or needing transportation—those kinds of things. Your parents have wisdom that can help you make your service even more helpful—and they can point out pitfalls you aren't aware of. Did you know, for example, that the girl with appendicitis probably can't have the chocolate you were planning to take to her? Your mom will know, and she can help you think of something else to take.

Step 5.

Make any necessary preparations. It might help to write them down here so you'll have a checklist. Just look at the service you want to perform and see if you need:

- supplies if you're going to make something.
- money if you're going to buy something.
- transportation if you need to go somewhere.
- a convenient time for the people you're going to serve (will they be home, will they be busy?).

Let's say you're going to rake leaves for the lady next door while she's recovering from surgery. You'll need:

- a rake and a wheelbarrow.
- someplace to pile the leaves or big bags to stuff them in.
- a time when the scrape, scrape, scrape of the rake won't bother her.

Write your prep notes here: _Cards_____
_____.

Step 6.

As you head into your service, think of a way that you can do this thing with as little fanfare as possible. The idea is not to draw attention to what you're doing. That doesn't mean you have to wear a bag over your head while you're raking the neighbor's leaves. It does mean doing it quietly without making a big announcement beforehand. It means getting the job done without looking around to see if passersby are noticing how wonderful you're being.

If you can pull it off, it's good to be anonymous so the person you're serving doesn't even know who did it. That doesn't work in every situation, like if you're going to entertain your little cousins while your aunt packs for a move. Write some ideas for how you can perform your service without getting attention for it:

_____
_____.

Step 7.

Do your thing! Enjoy it. Delight in it! After all, this is a God thing.

Step 8.

Afterward do two things:

1. Refuse any payment or reward of any kind if you can do it gracefully. Of course, if your uncle sends you flowers for walking his dog while he was laid up with a sprained ankle, don't throw them on his front porch! You can accept them graciously. But if your friend's mother wants to pay you for bringing your friend's homework to her every day while she was sick, you can simply say, "Really, Mrs. What's-It, I did it because I wanted to. I'd rather not take any money."

2. Write about your experience in your journal. Record what it felt like and how the people responded and how jazzed you are about doing more things for people. You'll discover that ideas will pop up all over the place and that some of them will be for things you can do on the spot— like stop that girl and zip up her backpack, which is hanging open and about to get dumped all over the hall. Yes, this is a discipline, but the idea of practicing a discipline is that eventually it will simply become part of who you are.

Girlz WANT TO KNOW

✿ *ZOOEY: Me first, because I've been dying to have this question answered since the first page of this chapter! What about my mom? She always thinks that if I do something for somebody else, I'm going to get hurt or something. I mean, honestly!*

She says I can't go on the Walk for the Hungry—you know, where you get people to pledge money for every mile you walk—because I'll get a cold. She wouldn't let me help serve a meal at Potter's House—even though practically our whole church is going—because it's in a bad part of town. She won't even give me permission to give some of my stuffed animals to the women's shelter, because she says I'll miss them in a few days and I'll be all bummed out. It makes me so mad, and I know some people think I'm just being selfish because I never help. What can I do?

First, you thank God for giving you a mom who loves you and wants to protect you. Yeah, it feels a little smothering right now, but you still need to count your blessings. Now—you do have a challenge here. You could start by sharing with her, in a respectful way, of course, what you've been learning in this book. Don't march into her room and say, "Mom, you don't have a clue about God's love. Let me just tell you something . . ." Pray for her in your quiet time.

Then don't fight with her about the things she has already forbidden you to do. Be alert for little services that your mom couldn't possibly object to. Some of them will just appear, and you'll be able to do them right then and there—like give your friend a Kleenex and someone to listen when she's crying at lunch or help your teacher carry her huge armload of stuff in from her car.

Others may require your mom's permission, but what can she say about your wanting to help your little brother with his homework (now *there's* a humbling experience!) or empty the dishwasher every night without being told? The key is to start with what's possible and let God accomplish what you can't.

❁ *SUZY: I watered all the outside plants for the lady across the street when she had to go out of town for a funeral. When she came back, she insisted on paying me. I mean, she stuck the money in my hand and closed my fingers over it! I feel bad about going home with the cash, but what could I do? I was too scared to say no.*

That's okay, Suzy. There comes a point where it would be rude to refuse payment. Tossing the money into the flower bed is out of the question! You can still continue your service attitude. Write her a thank-you note, telling her that you appreciate the money but you really did it because you wanted to help her.

Then think of somebody who could use that money. Could you drop it in the collection plate at church? Give it to your sister who is trying to save up for a mission trip she's going on next summer? Treat your friend to a milkshake at McDonald's because she needs cheering up? One service kind of leads to another, doesn't it? That's what makes it fun. Who knows, that money from Mrs. Neighbor might just be a God thing also.

❁ *LILY: I love this whole serving thing. I'm so jazzed when I get to do something for somebody, especially if I can do it in secret. And most of the time I get something out of it. Like the time I was in a play at church to raise money to help a family pay for an operation their little girl needed. I learned all this new stuff about acting and stage makeup and costumes. It was awesome— only I felt kind of guilty because it was supposed to be about that family, not me.*

What you do is always partly about you, Lily. You do the planning, the preparation, and the actual service—so you're all over the thing! If in the process you learn ways to develop your own gifts and potential for more service, that's definitely a God thing. Avoid these pitfalls:

- forgetting all about why you're performing the service in the first place
- drawing attention to your part in it
- not using what you've learned to do more things for other people
- never doing that particular thing again because you think you were too selfish
- failing to go to God with all your concerns, no matter what they are (after all, the answers are never more than a prayer away)

God wants you to find joy in life in spite of the sacrifices you sometimes have to make. Don't you think Jesus had fun when he was having those dinners with his friends? Who would have hung out with him if he hadn't been delightful to be with? He must have felt pretty good when a blind person walked away seeing because he healed him. If there had been no joy in what he did, nobody would have followed him. So you go, girl. Enjoy the services you perform and the benefits you get from them. They're all part of the God thing.

Talking to God About It

Do you have a calendar—or can you make a one-month calendar for yourself? In your quiet time for the next thirty days, pray that God will use you in service to other people, even in the smallest ways. Each night for those thirty days, write the result for that day on your calendar. What service did God give you to perform? At the end of your month, thank God for all those opportunities—and ask him for more!

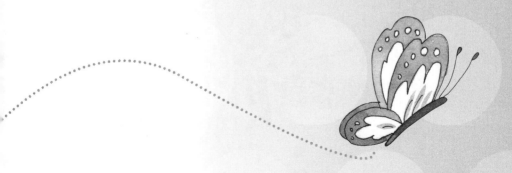

If I could give the biggest service ever, I would . . .

I Confess!

**Jesus said, "Receive the Holy Spirit.
If you forgive anyone his sins, they are forgiven."**
John 20:22–23

Before any of the Girlz even got to school one Monday morning, the following things happened:

- **Lily** called her younger brother an absurd little creep and told him she was never going to speak to him again.
- **Reni** pretended she didn't hear her mother calling her from downstairs, so she wouldn't have to talk to her hard-of-hearing great-grandmother on the phone.
- **Suzy** secretly gloated when she heard her parents yelling at her sister for making a bad grade. Suzy never makes bad grades.
- **Zooey** rolled her eyes at her mother when she told her to put on a warmer coat.
- **Kresha** hid her brother's homework so he couldn't find it, just to get back at him for spilling salsa all over hers the night before.

It wasn't even 8:00 a.m., and among the five of them, they'd broken half the Ten Commandments. What a rotten bunch of Girlz, huh?

Hmmm—would you say the same thing if you took a really honest, close look at your *own* day so far? Have you told a white lie today? Or let somebody believe something that wasn't true? Or called somebody a name, even in your mind? Or ignored someone who needed a hello? Or wished your teacher would be sick today, so you wouldn't have to take the geography test? Or anything at all like that?

Unless you haven't even gotten out of bed yet, you've probably done some of those things. But before you start feeling like some kind of major loser, know this: God has a plan for dealing with the ugly stuff you wind up doing or the good things you just plain don't do. And this will be no surprise to you—that plan involves a spiritual discipline.

In this chapter we're going to talk about the confession discipline. It's the way we can get even the worst part of our character to become a God thing.

HOW IS THIS A God Thing?

Jesus, being the Son of God, didn't have a whole lot to confess, because he basically never did anything wrong! But although he was the most perfect human being who ever lived, he was still human.

As we've mentioned before, he showed his very human side the night before he died, when he was in the Garden of Gethsemane (Matthew 26:39). He knew what God wanted him to do, but like any human, he didn't want to endure all the pain, loneliness, and humiliation he knew he was about to suffer. He used other words, but basically he said to his Father, "If there's any way at all, please get me out of this." Immediately, almost before he drew another breath, Jesus realized that would destroy God's great plan. So he gave himself back to his Father and promised to do whatever needed to be done.

The next day, when Jesus was enduring the beatings and was hung on the cross—the suffering he was dreading so much—he cried out, "My God, my God, why have you forsaken me?" (Matthew 27:46). Moments later he gave up his spirit to God and died.

You might say that if anybody had a reason to complain, it was Jesus under those circumstances. Who could blame him for asking for a different plan, or feeling as if he couldn't trust God anymore? And yet the minute he lost faith, he was all over it, owning up to it with God and moving forward in obedience.

So if we're going to live the way Jesus did, we have to do the same thing. When we know we've messed up, we need to follow the spiritual discipline of confession. We need to admit our failure to God *and* ask him to guide us to do the God thing instead. It isn't just a matter of saying "I'm sorry," even if we really mean it. Confession of anything that has separated us from God has to be followed by moving on to do better next time.

Jesus knew this was going to be a toughie for people, so he told a lot of stories to help us understand. One of them is about two sons whose father asked them to do something. One son said, "Sure, Dad" and then didn't do it. The other son said, "No way I'm doing that" but later changed his mind and went to do what his father asked. Jesus asked which one was the better son, and, of course, everybody picked the second one (Matthew 21:28–32).

It isn't what you say you're going to do that makes you a good person; it's what you actually do—even if it means admitting you were wrong, feeling genuinely bad about it, and going back and making it right. And the "making it right" isn't just for that particular instance. It's the determination not to let that same weakness cause you to make another mistake. If the second son really wanted to be and do right, he would learn to say "Sure, Dad" and go out immediately to do what his father asked.

There are three things involved in the spiritual discipline of confession:

1. You must admit that you did or said or thought something wrong—or didn't do or say something you should have (you messed up, okay?).
2. You must be truly sorry about it, rather than just saying you're sorry because it's the right thing to do.
3. You must make up your mind that you're going to work on whatever caused you to mess up that way—and that means working with God to make real changes in you (you can't go this alone, remember?).

Some of you might be asking, "What good did it do Jesus to confess that he didn't want to be crucified? God made him do it anyway!"

For Jesus the benefits weren't immediate, and most of the time they aren't for us either. But he did receive them and you will too. Here's what happens when you genuinely confess.

You're Forgiven

It's nice if the people involved will forgive you, but you can't control whether that happens or not. You can *always* count on God to forgive you. If you don't know the story of the prodigal son found in Luke 15:11–32, now would be a good time to read it.

It's the story of a son who rebels against his father and runs off to do his own thing. When his life is in shambles and he realizes he's made a huge mistake, the son goes back home, hoping his father will forgive him and take him in again. The best scene in the whole story is when the father sees his broken-down, messed-up son coming up the road. The man is filled with compassion and runs to meet him, hugging and kissing him.

While the son goes on and on about how he doesn't deserve to be a son, saying he would expect no more than to be a servant in his father's house, the father plans a coming-home party for him. Now, you may be saying to yourself, *Yeah, right. Like my parents are going to hug me and kiss me when I tell them I just blackened my little brother's eye.* Jesus is talking about God the Father. He's showing us how God reacts when we realize we've fouled everything up and come to him knowing we don't deserve a thing. God throws a party. He's just so glad to have you home again. That's what forgiveness is.

You Learn How Amazing God Really Is

When Jesus was teaching, the religious scholars and Pharisees—who were always trying to trick Jesus and make him look like a phony—brought a woman to him who had been caught red-handed with somebody else's husband. According to the Law of Moses, she should have been stoned to death. But Jesus said, "If any one of you is without sin, let him be the first to throw a stone at her" (John 8:7). Of course, nobody did, and they all tried to sneak away. And *then* Jesus forgave the woman—who really had been sinning, there's no doubt about that—and sent her on her way, telling her to leave her life of sin.

That woman saw firsthand how amazing God is and how much his forgiveness means. Not only did she escape death, but she also went away no longer feeling like some tramp. She was forgiven. Her bad life was over. She had the chance to make a better life now. God does that same thing for us. It's amazing how he can change us when we let him.

You Have the Guidance to Move On, Down a Better Path

Jesus said it over and over again to the people who came to him: "Go now and leave your life of sin" (John 8:11). But he didn't say, "I've forgiven you, so I expect you to be perfect from now on." He said, "Learn from me, for I am gentle and humble in heart, and you will find rest for your souls" (Matthew 11:29).

Now, you may be saying, "That was easy for those people back then. They could just follow him around and watch him!" But you can too. You're doing it as you practice the spiritual disciplines. You're spending time alone with God. You're talking to him. You're getting rid of the things in your life that block him from your view. You're serving his people. You're confessing all your wrongdoings and asking for help to do better. The more you do those things, the more clearly you'll hear God thoughts in your head and have God feelings in your body and sense God's presence in your soul. It happens gently and quietly and leads you to be the person you were created to be.

The purpose of this quiz is to help you find out what *form* of confession would work best for you and bring you the closest to God. There are no right or wrong answers!

Imagine that you have just had a huge blowup with your best friend and it doesn't look as if it's ever going to be the same with her again. Even though you're so angry with her that you could spit, you've been able to look at the whole thing and realize that you were no angel, either. You did your part to ruin the friendship, and you feel horrible about it—so horrible that you can't concentrate on that big school project you have coming up. Something has to be done, and that something is confession.

Which one of these ways to confess all your misery to God sounds like something you would most like to do (keeping in mind that confession is seldom pleasant, no matter how you do it)? Read them all and then put a little cross next to the one you choose.

_____ A. Get down on your knees in your quiet place and pour it all out to God. Speak out loud or whisper or cry, but get it out in a physical way. Write your confession in your journal if you need to, or draw God a picture of how ugly you feel. Stay in your quiet space until you feel a little more peaceful. That peace isn't just the way you feel after a good cry. It's God's forgiveness.

_____ B. Go to a Christian adult you really respect and trust. It could be your mom or dad or another relative, your youth pastor or Sunday school teacher—even another friend's mom. Ask if that person will hear you confess what's weighing you down. Then let it all go. Avoid putting anyone else down or making any excuses. You're getting down to the nitty-gritty of what your responsibility is in what has happened. Ask your "confessor" not to give you advice at this point (unless you really want it) but to simply help you ask God to forgive you, and to reassure you that you have his forgiveness.

_____ C. Tell your minister, pastor, or priest that you would like to make a confession. In a private place pour out your sin just as you would by yourself or to a friend. This ordained person will pray for you and with you until you begin to feel all that ugliness lift from you. He or she will reassure you that in God's mind it's over. You're forgiven. You don't have to drag your sin around with you anymore.

As we talk about your choice, please keep two things in mind:

1. No matter how you choose to practice the discipline of confession, it's God who forgives you, not the person who hears your confession. Even if an ordained person makes the sign of the cross over you and says you are "absolved," that person is just observing a sacrament, which is an outward sign to symbolize something God is doing. It's a way of giving you faith and helping you to understand that you've been forgiven, but it isn't necessary. The matter is still between you and God.

2. The way you confess won't always be the same. When it's something really big and it's making you feel heavy, confessing to an adult may be the way to go. If you've done some little thing that's bothering you,

asking for God's forgiveness on the spot, no matter where you are, is all it takes. And every day in your quiet time, you'll want to own up to all the things you've done and left undone that day that have kept you from being all God wants you to be. It's possible that the more mini-confessions you make, the fewer major ones you'll have to face!

If you put a cross next to choice *A*, you're probably a private person and can accomplish a lot on your own. It would only make sense for you to confess your sins that way too. It will make you feel really close to God. Just be careful of a couple of things:

1. Don't hide your shortcomings because you're so incredibly ashamed of them. Keeping secrets is not the same as merely wanting some privacy. If something is happening that involves another person who isn't as willing to change as you are, please tell an adult you trust.
2. Don't keep confessing the same thing over and over to God. If you can't seem to change, ask someone to help you. Maybe you want to stop exaggerating so people will pay attention to you when you talk, but you just keep doing it. Or perhaps you would love more than anything to stop yelling at your little sister, but the words just scream out of your mouth before you even think about them. Confessing is absolutely necessary, but so is changing your behavior. If you can't do it alone, get someone to help you.

If you put a cross next to choice *B*, you are a people person. You always feel your most secure and sure when you're with people you respect and love. It's one of the most wonderful things about you, so it figures that you would want to make your major confessions to another person. That's definitely a God thing. Just be careful about a couple of possible pitfalls:

1. If you find yourself going to your confessor once a week with a big problem, you might not be doing the work you need to be doing to change the behavior that makes you need to confess in the first place! If the person you confess to is someone other than one of your parents, tell

your parents what's going on with you. They might want to get you to someone who can really walk you through the challenges. After all, God doesn't want us to just confess—he wants us to change.

2. If you feel as if you can't confess anything without that special person hearing it, it could mean you're starting to depend too much on that person and not enough on God. Try to spend a little more time on confession during your quiet time, just giving the little things to God. Does that help you to do those little things less and less? Write it down if you have to! God wants it to be more and more and more about the two of you.

If you put a cross next to choice *C,* you might have been raised in what's called a more "liturgical" church, such as Episcopal, Catholic, or Lutheran. Or maybe you just appreciate doing things in a more formal way. Some Christians may think that rituals get in the way of communicating with God, but that isn't necessarily the case. Sacraments are designed to help a person better understand what God is doing, by using symbols. It's the reason Jesus washed his disciples' feet and called the bread and wine at the Last Supper his body and blood. It's why we have baptism and marriage ceremonies and funeral services.

Some churches simply observe more sacraments than others, and confession to an ordained person is one of them. They just provide the opportunity to confessin case you're dealing with something very troublesome and want to be able to "see" more clearly what God is doing. Confession of this kind can be very special. Just be careful about a few things:

1. Don't skip out of the church office thinking everything is taken care of and you can get back to life as usual. Formal confession is just a beginning. It provides an opportunity for you to make real changes in yourself. The process isn't complete until you talk to God and find out what he wants you to do about the situation and how he wants you to change.

2. Your confession has to be real and genuine. This is not the kind of thing you do because you're wondering what it's like! Just remember that confession is a serious thing, no matter how, when, and where you do it.

Just Do It

We've talked about why you need to confess your sins to God and ask for forgiveness. You now know some ways to do that. In time you'll see which one is most comfortable for you in your unique relationship with God. Now it's time to practice the third part of confession—the go-and-sin-no-more part. Although God makes it possible for you to do that, there are definitely things *you* will need in order to do well, to make good change happen in you. Let's get to it!

The Outside Path to Change

Step 1.

Think of something you confessed—or should have confessed—to God recently. Your best choice (since we all have so many things to pick from!) is something you've done more than once, like a habit. Here are some examples to get your thoughts stirred up:

- telling little lies
- being less than kind to a sibling
- disrespecting your parents
- gossiping
- name calling
- wishing something bad would happen to somebody
- bragging
- using other people's stuff without permission
- whining
- begging for things from your parents
- putting people down
- cheating
- acting selfishly

- trying to get attention
- breaking promises

If you're sure this book is safe from prying eyes, write your "confessable thing" here (otherwise write it in your journal or some other safe place):

_____

_____

_____

Step 2.

If you haven't already gone to God with this sin and said, "God, I did this and I keep doing it. But I'm really sorry and I want to change," do that as soon as you can. Don't go any further with this until you have. Otherwise it's like doing exercises with a broken leg.

Step 3.

There are several things you can do to keep yourself from continuing to do wrong things while you and God are working on making changes. The following suggestions will help you—but they aren't the final solution, so keep that in mind as you work. Put a check next to each one that fits your situation, and start doing it today!

_____Stay away from the people who do the things you are trying to stop doing, even if they're friends.

_____Stay away from the places where you're most likely to do the things you're trying to stop doing—like the girls' bathroom when everyone is gossiping or that corner of the lunchroom where you tend to make fun of other people with your friends.

_____Get alone if you feel yourself wanting to do the thing you're trying to stop doing—such as when you want to flush your brother down the toilet or talk back to your mom.

_____The minute you want to do the thing you want to stop doing, start praying silently—when the test papers are passed out and you are tempted to cheat, when you see those cute shoes in the store and want to start begging your mom for them. What sin does is to separate you from God. It's hard to be separated from God while you're talking to him.

_____Ask an adult or a really good friend to signal you when he or she sees you falling into that old pattern. Your teacher could clear her throat (loudly!) when you start waving your hand wildly in the air to get attention, or your best friend could shake her head when she hears you start to brag. Then it's up to you to put on the brakes.

_____Carry some kind of reminder. If you tend to exaggerate when you're talking to your friends at the lunch table, put a note in your lunch box that says, "Keep it honest." If you usually scream at your brother when he bangs on the door to come into your room, put a sign on the back of your door that says, "Thank you for not yelling."

The Inside Path to Change

That's the outside path. Now let's work on the inside *while* you're doing the above. Sound like a lot of work? It is, but just keep in mind that you're not alone and keep praying. Try these things to find out what it is inside you that pushes your sin button. But please remember this: *If you can't change behavior that's causing you to mess things up for yourself and other people, get an adult you trust to help you.* It doesn't mean you're an idiot or you can't change. Some things just run a little deeper. That's why God made parents—to help you be the best person you can be.

With that in mind, start working on your issues on your own:

Step 1.

Think back to the last time you did the thing you're trying to change and write it here: _____.

Step 2.

Now think about what you were feeling just before you did it. Write it here: _____.

If that's confusing to you, maybe some examples will help.

"Just before I cheated on the spelling test, I got really anxious because I was so afraid I was going to get a bad grade and get in trouble with my parents."

"Right before I started saying bad stuff about Jennifer, I just felt so jealous because Molly, my best friend, was saying how nice Jennifer was and how she wanted to get to know her. And before I felt jealous, I felt scared—scared that Molly was going to start liking Jennifer more than me."

"The very second before I yelled at my brother and told him he was a pig and I never wanted him in my room again, I just felt this anger taking over. I hate it when he comes in my room and messes up my stuff. I feel like I don't have any privacy at all, and that makes me *so* mad!"

Go back and see *where* that feeling came from. In our examples, cheating came from anxiety, and anxiety came from fear of getting in trouble with parents. Backstabbing came from jealousy, and jealousy came from fear of being replaced in a friendship. Yelling and name-calling came from anger, and anger came from the frustration of never having any privacy. Write down where *your* feeling came from. It might help to do it this way: "When I did _____, I felt _____ before I did it, because of _____." That last thing you wrote is the thing you want to work on. If you talk to God about it, he will do his part. This is your part:

• Name that feeling or situation as soon as it arises. Admit to it. Say to yourself, *Here comes that whole fear thing about grades again.* Or *I'm so afraid Molly's going to find another best friend.* Or *I want privacy so badly, I can taste it!* Write what you'll say to yourself here:

_____

- Decide—ahead of time—if there's someone you can go to for help in changing that feeling or situation. Could you talk to your parents about how hard it is for you to live up to their expectations about grades and ask them for help with studying and homework? Could you tell your best friend how much her friendship means to you? Could you talk to your parents about your room being off-limits to your brother? Write that person's name here: _____.
Think about what you might say and write it here:
_____. (And don't worry about what that person will say—you can't control that anyway.)

- Figure out if there's something *you* could do differently to squelch that feeling or situation. Could you study more so you don't get anxious about tests? Could you develop some other friendships so your whole social life doesn't revolve around one friend? Could you invite your brother in at certain times to share a bag of popcorn or play a game of checkers so he isn't so eager to sneak into your inner sanctum when you don't want him there? If you can think of something, write it here:

_____.

- Is there something physical or creative that you could do to work through feelings of frustration and anger and fear? What about kicking a soccer ball around or writing furiously about it in your journal or drawing a picture of it in big, bold strokes? Wouldn't it help to ride your bike as fast as you can or throw a Frisbee for your dog or do twenty somersaults in the backyard? Or how about a poem on the subject—or a sculpture made from Play Dough that you call "Angry" or "Afraid." These are called outlets. An outlet isn't a solution, but it puts you in a frame of mind so you *can* reach a solution. No one can change when she's angry or frustrated or afraid. Those feelings just make you want to react—and that's why you sin in the first place! Write a possible outlet here:

_____.

- Now go back and *do* what you've planned. It could take a while. It will definitely take some courage. But that's what discipline is, right? And you're getting so good at it!

Girlz WANT TO KNOW

❀ *ZOOEY: You know, I wouldn't be so tempted to act like someone I'm not if Ashley and those other girls didn't make fun of me so much when I'm being who I am. Don't get me wrong, I'm confessing every day about what a phony I am sometimes, but how come God doesn't work on them instead of just on me?*

Actually, Zooey, what God does with others is between God and them. That was one of the last things Jesus said to his disciples before he went back to heaven. Jesus gave Peter some instructions, but Peter pointed to another disciple and said, "Lord, what about him?" Jesus answered, "What is that to you? You must follow me" (John 21:21–22). It isn't that you shouldn't be concerned for other people, but when it comes to God showing you what he wants you to do, your job is to do it and not get involved in what other people are supposed to do.

That's not all. It sounds as if you're working on your own stuff, but you're still blaming other people for "making you do it" or at least making you think you have to do it. Just as you can't control what other people are doing, they really can't control what you're doing, either. You *always* have a choice about what you're going to do, what you're going to say, and how you're going to respond. Ashley and her friends can't take that choice away from you. What is their weapon? Words. Words hurt, that's true. Walk away so you can't hear their words. Fill your head with your own words: *God loves me. God made me to be me. God can help those girls if they'll let him. God is helping me right this minute.*

❁ *SUZY: I don't want to sound stuck-up or anything, but I can't think of any sin that I commit all the time. I make good grades and I have nice friends. I never get in trouble at school, and I don't do anything to upset my parents. I guess I'm kind of a boring person when it comes to sin, because I don't have anything to confess!*

First of all, Suzy, there is nothing boring about a good person. Just having such a trouble-free life makes you fascinating! But don't confuse "never getting into any kind of trouble" with "never sinning." You can do the first one, but you can't pull off that second one. You're human and all humans make mistakes. Admitting that is a confession in itself.

Now, we're not out to make you dig into yourself to try to dredge up something! But it's important to make extra-special sure that you aren't ignoring something that's separating you from God. For instance, what do you do to keep from getting in trouble in absolutely every area of your life? Do you sometimes hold back things you'd really like to say—about an unfair grade or a harsh rule, maybe? Do you stress out over those grades? Do you get upset when everything isn't perfect? Those don't sound like bad things, and they really aren't, but they do separate you from God. What happened to trusting God, especially when you've done your best?

So don't look for things that aren't there, but be alert for things that keep you from being the real you. Notice when you feel nervous or stiff or self-conscious. Pay attention to the things God can help you with so the two of you can be closer and you can be freer. Freedom to be who you are—that's what confession gives you. You wouldn't want to miss out on that, would you?

❁ *RENI: I picked choice "B", and I really want to confess something to another person, but I don't know who. My mom and dad are great, but this is about them and how I treat them sometimes, so I think it should be some other adult. How do I know who to choose?*

You are very wise not to go to your parents with your confession. You'll probably want to talk to them about things eventually as you do your "Just Do It" activities, but to be completely honest in your confession, you'll want what we call a third party—someone who isn't involved.

Here are some things to look for in a confessor. While you're looking for someone who has these qualities, keep praying. If this is a God thing, he will provide someone for you. But just as always, you have to do some of the work! Look for:

- someone who is a Christian.
- someone who is an adult.
- someone who can be trusted not to share your confession with anybody else.
- someone who is understanding and has shown compassion.
- someone who seems to love being a Christian.
- someone who has his or her life together as far as you can see.
- someone who is a person you would go to for advice.
- someone who has a sense of humor.

Don't forget to get permission to meet with this person. If your parents ask why, be honest. Don't let fear that they'll say no cause you to do something sneaky. Then you'll have something else to confess!

✿ *LILY: I've been working with God on the way I boss people around all the time, and I'm getting better. I know I'm forgiven for the times I've hurt people's feelings and made them feel like losers. But even though I don't do it anymore—well, as much—I still feel so bad about myself. I can't get rid of that.*

You're absolutely right that God has forgiven you—and good for you for working on your bossiness. Those lingering bad feelings are there because deep down inside, you don't really believe that God has completely wiped your slate clean. Aside from talking to God about it, you might try one or more of the following suggestions to help you accept God's forgiveness.

- Write down all the times you can think of when you were bossy and hurt someone's feelings or gave them a reason to be mad. And try to keep it to one page, Lily—we know how you are! Once you have it all written down, ask God to help you accept his forgiveness. Then tear that paper into the tiniest pieces you can and throw them into the trash can or the fireplace. Watch them go away. It might help you to "see" that your sins are gone.

- When it seems appropriate (not in the lunch line, for example), apologize to anyone you've hurt or stifled. Just one time—and it doesn't have to be a dramatic scene. Simply say something like, "I know  I was really bossy when we were working on that history project together. I'm sorry if I hurt your feelings." That's it. It's possible that the person will then give you a list of every time you got to her with your bossiness, but you don't have to respond to that. One more "I'm sorry" is all you need to say. Most people, however, will appreciate your apology and say something like, "Oh, that's okay." Maybe it wasn't then, but it is now, and you can let it go.

- Remember that Jesus died to *take away your sins*. When you're praying about this heavy thing you're still carrying around inside you, picture yourself giving this bundle or package of sin to God and picture him taking it. In your imagination look at the space you just emptied and ask God what he's going to fill it with. Picture that space filling up with light or warmth or chocolate (which *of course* symbolizes love!). Do that as many days as you need to and see what happens. God's very patient about taking sin from you over and over, no matter how many times you ask for it back. And you can never take it all the way back, because God's in there trying to fill up the space!

Talking to God About It

Stop reading for a moment and write a letter to God. Tell him all about the thing that keeps separating you from him. You'll want to do this on a piece of paper instead of here in your book. Once you write it, with all the details, we suggest that you take it to your special place at quiet time, get real with God, and present it to him with the most heartfelt "I'm sorry." Then destroy that piece of paper, because you don't need it anymore. The sin it describes is in God's hands now. So cut it into pieces or rip it up or put it in your dad's shredder (with permission) or crumple it up and toss it into the fire in the fireplace (again, with permission). (It's best not to try to flush it down the toilet!) Then enjoy a few minutes with God, thanking him for taking that off your hands and asking him to help you with whatever it is that makes it so easy for you to slide into that sin.

The absolute worst thing I ever did in my life was . . .

_____

_____

_____

_____

_____

_____

_____

_____

_____

_____

Going All Out for God

**True worshipers will worship the Father in spirit and truth,
for they are the kind of worshipers the Father seeks.**
John 4:23

When **Reni** found out that the last spiritual discipline we'd be learning about was worshiping and celebrating God, she said, "Whew! Finally one I'm already doing! I go to church every Sunday and most Wednesdays. I think I'm covered on this worship thing."

But hey, if just showing up at church were all it took to worship, we wouldn't need a whole chapter to talk about it. We could sum it up in one sentence!

Since you *are* about to read a whole chapter on worshiping God and celebrating all that he's doing in your life, you're probably guessing there's more to it than that—and you're right. It's great stuff that you aren't going to want to miss. The Girlz are glad they didn't.

Lily used to yawn through church about half the time. Now she actually looks forward to going.

Suzy didn't want to go to church, until Lily and Reni practically bribed her. She thought they'd be doing something she didn't know how to do and she'd feel embarrassed. Funny how she now joins right in as if she's been doing it all her life!

Zooey always wanted to go to church, especially after she got to be friends with the Girlz. When she did finally get permission from her mom to go, to tell the truth she was a little disappointed that nobody had a miraculous healing at the altar or something. Then she learned what worship and celebration were really about.

Worship is so obviously about God, it seems as though it would be pointless to even discuss the question, "How is this a God thing?" in our book—except that what we *think* worship is and what it *really* is might be two entirely different things. We need to make sure we know the difference before we can worship God's way. After all, the church didn't change to help Lily, Suzy, and Zooey love worship more. *They* were the ones who changed.

They started by understanding *why* God wants us to worship. That's a good place for you to begin, as well.

HOW IS THIS A God Thing?

So what *is* worship, exactly?

If you gave the first answer that came into your mind, you might say something about going to church to sing songs and listen to a sermon.

You'd be partly right. Those are some of the *ways* we worship.

But worship itself is what's happening inside you when you're singing and praising and listening to a sermon. Jesus never talked about the ways to worship. Instead he told us about the happening-inside stuff:

"Worship the Lord your God, and serve him only," he said (Matthew 4:10). That means that when you go to church, it's your chance to make it all about God rather than all about you. Instead of having to worry about what you're wearing or whom you're sitting with or whom you're not sitting with or whether you're singing like a foghorn, you can focus on God. It's easier in church than it is any other place, because you don't have the phone ringing and homework beckoning. God wants that time with you.

"But don't I have that in my quiet time?" you may ask. You do, but Jesus goes on to say that God wants you to focus on him while you're shoulder to shoulder with *other* people who are focusing on him at the same time. "Where two or three come together in my name," Jesus said, "there am I with them" (Matthew 18:20).

If two or three can feel the Lord's presence when they're together, what about twenty or thirty? Or two or three hundred? Think about it this way— what's the difference between going to McDonald's and a movie all by yourself and going with a friend? There's definitely more good energy and more reasons to laugh and feel good when you go with your friend, right? And what happens when you go with *all* your friends? The energy goes through the roof! You're laughing for days!

Yeah, sometimes you like to do things alone, and at other times you want some alone time with your best friend. But hanging out with a crowd of Girlz who enjoy the same things you do fills you with friendship and gets you jazzed about life. It's the same with getting together with a group of people who share your beliefs and want to sing and talk and pray about them all at the same time. Your daily quiet time with God helps you develop your relationship with him. Your worship with other God-believers helps you to know how important that is.

Just to make sure we really understood what he meant by gathering together in his name, Jesus put his disciple Simon Peter in charge of forming his church. "I tell you that you are Peter, and on this rock I will build my church," Jesus said to him, because the name  Peter means "rock" (Matthew 16:18). So we need to worship in the church together so we can feel the strength of Jesus under our feet. We know we have something to stand on, to base our beliefs and our behavior on. Sure beats floating around out there never quite knowing who we are or what we're supposed to be doing! A rock beneath us gives us more security than shifting ground below us.

Jesus also meant for worship in the church to protect us from the evil stuff that exists in the world. "The gates of Hades will not overcome it," he said (Matthew 16:18). That's because when you have a whole church full of people standing beside you, believing what you believe, it makes you feel stronger. Then you can go out and stand up to the daily bullying and teasing and snobbery and meanness—and the temptation to involve yourself in any of those—because you have worshiped God with people who are willing to support you. What more reason do you need?

Just Do It

There are very few Christians who don't believe we need to worship together. The Bible says that Jesus was constantly in the temple. The differences start to happen when we realize that there are a lot of different *ways* to worship. The important thing is that no matter how our worship looks, we all include the same basic things.

Jesus showed us those things in *his* worship. As you begin to practice the spiritual discipline of worship, you'll want to make sure you're including the following things (we've set them up like activities so you can do them one at a time until they just become part of you).

Worship Activity 1

If you don't already belong to a church, you'll want to find one. That's what God wants. He *looks* for people to come and be with his other believers. "A time is coming and has now come," Jesus said, "when the true worshipers will worship the Father in spirit and truth, for they are the kind of worshipers the Father seeks" (John 4:23). Your reading this book means that God is seeking you—asking you to come.

If you were an adult, that would be easy, right? You could just get in the car and go! But since you still depend on other people for transportation and you still need to get permission and all those other kid things, your choices may seem kind of limited. Don't throw up your hands and say, "Nah, I'll wait until I get my driver's license." Try this approach:

1. **Pray.** God wants you to have a church—we've settled that. So don't you think he's going to help you find one you can get to?

2. **Talk to your parents.** Ask them if they'll take you to a church they can enjoy. Sometimes it takes a kid to get an adult back into the arms of the church. That would be a good service for you!

3. **If that doesn't help,** ask if you can have permission to go to church or even a youth night with a friend. In most churches worship goes on every time its members get together. If your folks are afraid that if they let you go, someone will come knocking on their door, pressuring them to come, ask your friend's parents to reassure them that this isn't going to happen.

4. **That means finding a friend** who goes to an active, loving church. If none of your close friends are churchgoers, now would be a good time to expand your friendships a little! It's pretty lonely to have a life in God when there is no one close to you who supports you and is on her own journey with our Lord. It can be done of course, but God would so much rather have us bonding with other God-lovers along the way.

5. **Once you start attending church,** sit down with God in your quiet time and make a commitment to him that you will be part of his church and worship there every week. Then every day in your quiet time make that promise again and ask for God's help in keeping it. (Have you figured

out by now that you can't do a whole lot without your quiet time with God?) Write the name of your church here:

_____.

You might want to add how God got you there (whether you just started or you've been going since you were in diapers):

_____.

Worship Activity 2

Get yourself ready in some way before the worship service starts. Without some preparation it's hard—almost impossible!—to snap right from the world of homework and brothers and the dreaded cafeteria food to the world of focusing on God. Here are some suggestions to get you started. (Obviously, you don't have to do all of them, or you'd never even get to church!)

1. **The night before,** start talking to God about your upcoming worship while you lay out your clothes or take your bath. Make those activities special times for you and God as you think about looking your best in his honor or letting him wash away your sins.
2. **Get ready as quickly as you can Sunday morning** so you have time to read the Bible lesson for the day (most churches announce that beforehand). That way you can get a head start on things you don't understand. It's amazing how if you've already studied something, it's more interesting to hear about it again.
3. **When you get inside the church,** sit very still and pray silently before the service starts, instead of twisting around to see who's there or focusing on your little sister, who's climbing under the seat. Thank God that you're there. Let go of anything that's nagging you and might keep you from concentrating. Notice all the people sitting in front of you and pray for them—maybe just in general or perhaps even in detail. Does that older lady look lonely in that pew by herself? Do you see a family that has a sick grandma someplace far away? Do you *really* want

your sister to get out from under the seat and behave? Take it all to God while you have this quiet chance.

4. **Notice how the church is all ready for worship.** Are there flowers up front? Candles lit? Does the whole place smell pleasantly of furniture polish? Is there music playing? Banners hung? Sun streaming through stained-glass windows? Rain chattering on the metal roof? Tell God how much you appreciate everyone who goes to so much trouble to make everything beautiful for worship—including him.

Worship Activity 3

In most churches worship involves music, prayer, readings from the Bible, and some kind of sermon or talk that helps bring understanding to the readings. Make sure you participate in those as much as you can, rather than just sitting back waiting to be entertained. Church worship is the kind of thing that *isn't* going to be fun or interesting if you aren't in there *doing* it. It isn't like watching a video!

Jesus really got into it when he went to the temple to worship—even though that was a pretty dull scene. Someone read from the Scriptures, which most people didn't seem to understand, and then some scholar would stand up and explain it, which only seemed to confuse everyone more. Talk about boring!

But Jesus didn't just sit there and yawn through it. He stood up and taught, and people sat up and took notice. Can't you just imagine the scene (Mark 1:22), people nudging each other awake from their catnaps and whispering, "Who *is* this guy? He sounds like he actually knows what he's talking about!"

Before you start getting nervous—or excited!—about jumping up in church and launching into a mini-sermon, relax. We're not suggesting that you literally do what Jesus did. What we're saying is that to fully understand it all, you have to be part of what's going on. Here are some ways you can do that.

1. **Join in the singing.** It doesn't matter whether you have a voice like an opera star or you sound like a bullfrog. This isn't an audition for the school musical—this is a chance to praise God with everything

you have. In most churches words are provided, so you aren't expected to already know the songs by heart, and the music itself is generally pretty to sing to. Nobody is going to notice if you sing the wrong notes and just kind of mumble along at first. It's letting it loose for God that counts. You'll never know the powerful feeling that runs through your veins after you've been singing all-out praise, until you try. It's a feeling that stays with you for a long time (and coaxes you to continue in the shower later!).

2. **Pray right along with the leader.** That means listening carefully and imagining God hearing those words at the same time you do. Picture God nodding and smiling and even crying some. It also means whispering or even saying out loud your own prayers when the time is right. You may hear people around you murmuring, "Yes, Jesus" as the prayers are being offered, and that's okay too—as long as it's coming naturally to you. Sticking a "Yes, Jesus" in there like punctuation because you think that's what you're supposed to do won't make you feel closer to God.

3. **Get into the Bible reading,** just the way you're doing in your quiet time. If you have to, close your eyes so you won't be distracted by the kid in front of you who's running a Tonka truck over the back of the pew. Picture the scene. Imagine Jesus or the prophet or whoever is talking. If there are things you don't understand, jot them down on your bulletin or try to remember them so you can ask somebody about them later. The sermon usually clears up a lot of things.

4. **Listen to the sermon.** Sometimes that's easier said than done. Let's face it, some preachers' sermons are a real snore. But even if you don't have the funniest, most fascinating pastor up there in the pulpit, try to gather what you can that applies to you, even if it's just one sentence. If you find yourself getting squirmy, get as still as you can and silently ask God to help you focus on something that's being said that you can take home with you. (This is definitely not the time for a resounding "Yes, Jesus!")

Worship Activity 4

Then—just let it happen. You're probably saying, "Uh, *what? What does that* mean?"

What it means is that worship isn't something you *do*. It's something that *happens* while you're singing, praying, and listening together with other people who are seeking God.

Remember when we talked about Jesus getting up in the temple and making everything clear to the people? That was the start of God changing the idea of worship. It went from being something like school to being a chance to connect with God. It's like the difference between just studying for a test to get a good grade and suddenly realizing that you've actually learned something you're always going to remember.

So what does that feel like—that "true worship in spirit and truth" Jesus was talking about?

It's one of the mysteries of God and it's different for everyone, but here are some of the ways you can know that something is *happening* between the two of you. Remember that nobody feels all of them—and certainly not all at once!

1. **God seems real and close** instead of like some unreachable king sitting on a lofty throne handing down commands you might not want to obey.
2. **You realize way down inside you** that God totally loves you like nobody else does—that he accepts you, wants to help you, and forgives all the rotten things you do.

3. **You feel free inside.** Nothing is weighing on your mind. At that moment you aren't dragged down by what other people think of you or expect from you.

4. **You have the urge to confess** things to God so there's nothing standing between you and him.

5. **You suddenly want to sing** more praise songs because you're so filled with love for God.

6. **You understand something in the Bible** that never made sense to you before. You're jazzed about it.

7. **You want to do something good** for someone else. You start itching to serve.

8. **You start listening for the God whispers,** and you really believe you'll hear them—no matter how God decides to give them to you.

9. **You stop squirming** at the thought of that word *obey.* You *want* to do whatever God asks of you.

10. **You feel love for everyone** who is gathered in the church to worship with you, even though you don't know every one personally.

11. **You feel like part of a church family,** and you take that warm feeling of belonging with you when you leave to go on with your week.

12. **You don't feel alone** and separate and different from everyone else.

There is no activity you can do to *make* any of these things happen. They come from God and nowhere else. The spiritual discipline of worship—all the things we've talked about in our "Just Do It" section—is the way to get yourself to a place and a time and a frame of mind in which you can let God bring you those wonderful thoughts and feelings.

Worship Activity 5

Once you leave the church, *act* on anything you've learned, realized, or felt while you were there. It's not like a movie after which you can just walk out feeling good. God has given you some instructions. It's time to obey them. Here's a way to do that:

1. **As soon as you can, have some quiet time**—it may even be in the back of the car on the way home from church. Think of one thing God seemed

to be saying to you in church. God speaks in a lot of different ways. It could have come from the Bible reading or the words to one of the songs or the way you felt when you saw that young boy in the wheelchair. If this is hard for you, pick the one thing about the whole service that has stayed in your mind, even if it's how amazed you were at how much money was in that collection plate. The Girlz have some examples for you:

Lily: I had this rush of being sorry for always yelling at my younger brother. It wasn't like I thought, *I shouldn't be doing that.* I felt like I wanted to apologize to him right then—and I *never* apologize to my brother! I think that's what God wants me to do.

Reni: There was a person playing the harp today during the service, and I loved that, being a musician myself. Then I thought, *Wow—I just play my violin for school and city orchestra and stuff like that. I never play it just for God. Maybe that's what God wants me to do.*

Suzy: There's a place in the service where we're supposed to turn to each other and shake hands or hug and say something like, "God's peace be with you." I hate that part because I'm pretty shy, and I usually pretend like I have to blow my nose or dig in my purse for collection money. But today this lady in front of me turned around and grabbed both my hands and just, like, looked into my eyes. I had to look at her. I didn't have a choice. But I didn't feel funky or weird or anything. It was kind of nice. So—is God telling me to start looking people in the eye, you know, like work on my shyness?

2. **As soon as you can,** write down what you think God was asking you to do and put it in a place where you'll see it at least once a day. Maybe you put it in your talking-to-God journal or on a piece or paper you can stick up on your bulletin board. Don't write it on your hand unless you don't plan to wash it for a week!

3. **Each day during the week,** do some little thing to obey what God has asked you to do. You don't have to do it all at once—sometimes things take time. But each day do some small piece of it. Here's what the Girlz did:

Lily asked her brother if he wanted to watch a movie with her that afternoon. She said he could pick the movie (always a scary thing to do!), and she would make the microwave popcorn. He was a little suspicious, but there was food involved, so he said okay. While she was dumping the popcorn into two bowls, Lily prayed that God would help her know how to do this apology thing. She wasn't quite sure how to approach it. During the movie Joe did his usual annoying stuff like touching her with his smelly feet and tossing the occasional piece of popcorn at her. She definitely didn't feel like apologizing to him *then*, but she just kept remembering her prayer—and she couldn't yell at him, either. So she didn't. It was a start.

Reni went through her music that afternoon to see if there were any worship pieces in there. She didn't find any. She got the church organist's phone number from her mom so she could call her and ask her for suggestions.

Suzy tried *not* looking down every time the teacher looked at her the next day in school. At first it was funky because she wasn't used to it, but about the third time, she saw that the teacher was actually smiling at her. Suzy smiled back. Maybe this wasn't so difficult after all.

4. **During the week** keep working on doing what God asked you to do. When you have quiet time, ask God how you're doing. You might want to write a sentence in your journal every day or give yourself a star on your calendar to mark your progress. If you see that you're falling down on the job, confess that to God and get going again. Change is hard, but if you don't change as the result of worshiping God, you aren't really worshiping. Don't be bummed out, though. You and God both want it to happen. You're both working on it. So it will happen.

✓ CHECK Yourself OUT

Those are the basics of worship, no matter what the worship service looks like. Remember when we discussed that there are different *ways* to worship? Those ways weren't important to Jesus. He never told us exactly how to put together a church service. He left that up to us because all of us are different and we connect with God in different ways. There are so many wonderful possibilities that it makes the expression of our faith very rich.

Right now you're probably going to the church your parents have picked or the one that's available to you through friends or relatives. If you worship the way we've talked about, you'll have a wonderful experience. But as you get older, you'll realize that you have choices. You'll want to be sure you make a church choice that allows your worship to draw you closer to God.

These are some things to consider:

Do the people in the church believe as you do?

Do you feel at home there?

Do you know that God is sending you to that church for some reason?

Do you enjoy the worship service?

The last question is one thing you can start thinking about now, so let's find out what you're drawn to.

As you're taking this little survey, keep in mind that some people have strong feelings about whether we should pray any prayers out of a book or how often we should have Communion. We respect those strong feelings. Our quiz is just designed to see what *your* feelings are. Your relationship with God along the way will tell you how to act on them.

So here are the possibilities for worship. Enjoy looking at them and seeing what might make you feel closest to God. Circle the letter that best fits you in each set.

Music

   A. Lots of praise music, maybe with a praise team up front and guitars and drums. I want to feel free to clap and raise my hands and really sing out.

   B. Simple hymns that you just sing with the piano or the organ. I like the old familiar songs, like the ones my grandmother sings around the house—that kind of thing.

   C. Stately, majestic music like on a pipe organ. It's all really big. I get chills when I hear that kind of music for God.

Prayer

   A. The pastor or the leader offers a prayer that just comes from his heart. And then other people in the congregation join in. You hear people saying, "Amen" and "Yes, Lord," so it's like everybody's in on it.

   B. Everyone reads some prayers together, and the leader prays some just on his own. It's all very quiet and simple and respectful.

   C. All the prayers are in a book and they're beautiful. It's like everything you've always wanted to say to God and didn't have the words. Some the minister reads alone, and some everyone reads together. In a few places the congregation is invited to offer prayers out loud. That's done very reverently.

Bible Readings

A. The Bible is quoted through the whole service. The Scripture the preacher is going to base his sermon on is definitely read. And during the sermon people have their Bibles open so they can look up the passages the preacher is talking about. You get the feeling that the people who have been worshiping there for a while really know the Bible—even the kids.

B. One or more passages from the Bible are read, and the preacher will base the sermon on one. The preacher really tries to apply the Bible to people's lives in the sermon.

C. Each week several passages from the Bible are read—a psalm, an Old Testament reading, a New Testament reading other than from a Gospel, and a Gospel reading. Members of the congregation come up and read them, except the Gospel portion, which is usually read by the minister. Sometimes something special is done around the Gospel reading, like a song, or maybe the minister walks down the aisle to read the Gospel in the midst of the people.

Sermon

A. The sermon is the main part of the service, the thing everybody waits for. The preacher talks about some part of the Bible and gives background so everyone can understand it. Then he shows how people can *live* what the Bible says. Like Jesus, the preacher will use stories to make things clearer—and sometimes even jokes. Don't be surprised to see the preacher using props or even showing slides. It's lively and inspiring.

B. The sermon is an important part of the service, so everyone gets still and quiet, expecting the preacher to make God's Word clear. It depends on the preacher, of course, but this is usually a calm talk that simply gives the people things to think about on their own. You might see heads nodding in agreement, but you probably won't hear a lot of "Amen's"!

C. The sermon is only one part of the service, so it only lasts about fifteen minutes. It usually happens right after the reading of the Gospel, because the preacher often talks about the Gospel in the sermon. Depending on the preacher, it can be a lively talk that gets people stirred up, or it can be simply a food-for-thought kind of thing. It's usually formal but quite warm at the same time.

The "Decorations"

A. The church looks alive! There may be flowers, banners, or pictures on a big screen. It's colorful and inviting, and it seems to be moving, even when everyone is sitting still. It creates excitement about God.

B. The church is simple but beautiful. There may be a few things that remind us of God, like a cross or some candles. For the most part it invites people to focus totally on God from the moment they walk in.

C.. The church is an artistic expression of faith. The building itself may have a steeple and/or stained-glass windows. The altar at the front focuses your attention, and there is always a cross and usually candles and flowers. The whole church seems to say to you, "This is a sacred place, different from all the other places in your life. Let yourself be in God's presence here, where it is easy, so you can continue to be in his presence in the world, where it is difficult."

Communion

A. The service of Holy Communion is celebrated at various times throughout the year, and it is a lovely, special time for remembering what Jesus taught us—that we are to be so connected to God through him that it's as if we're living in his body and have his blood running through our veins. The body and blood are symbolized by special crackers or bread and juice.

B. The service of Holy Communion is celebrated four times a year or even once a month. There is structure to the service, so the people feel as if they're right there at the table with Jesus during the last dinner he had with his disciples. Sometimes bread is used and sometimes special crackers are used to symbolize Jesus' battered and crucified body. Juice represents his blood that was spilled out on the ground for our sins. A special feeling exists among all the people who are celebrating their unity with Jesus Christ in this way. It's like being at supper with people who love you, even though they don't know you.

C. The service of Holy Communion (or the Eucharist, as it is also called) is celebrated at least once a month, if not every week. It's the central part of the worship service, and everything else leads up to it. It's done in a formal, special way. The minister (called the Celebrant) "acts out" what Jesus did at his last supper with his disciples, lifting up the cup of wine and giving thanks, then

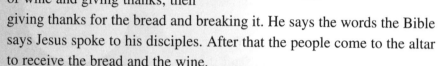

giving thanks for the bread and breaking it. He says the words the Bible says Jesus spoke to his disciples. After that the people come to the altar to receive the bread and the wine.

The bread may be real bread or special wafers. The blood is symbolized by wine and is offered in a common cup that everyone drinks out of (somebody wipes it off after each person drinks!). People don't *have* to take Communion every Sunday to be doing it "right." It's simply offered as a way to connect with God—one of many ways in our lives.

If you circled mostly *A*s, you are drawn to a lively church that has today-type music and a lot going on during the service. You like to be really involved in the service and have a chance to express the feelings that bubble up inside you. You'll find that kind of worship in most nondenominational churches, as well as in what we call "mainline denominations" that are Bible centered. The Baptist Church would be an example. If you don't already go to a church like that but would like to experience one, find out if any of your friends go to that type of church. Then ask your parents if they would mind if you visited. It isn't that you're going to suddenly insist that the whole family change churches! You just want to open yourself up to other forms of worship. They all lead us to the same God through Jesus.

If you circled mostly _B_s, you're attracted to a quiet, simple type of worship. It has some structure, so you always know what to expect, but it gives you a chance to quietly apply what Jesus taught to the way you live your life. It doesn't sound boring to you—it sounds peaceful. It sounds as if it could really inspire you. If you don't already go to a church like this—Methodist, for example, or some Presbyterian churches—follow the same suggestions we gave under _A_. A visit can even be a good way to better understand your friends who attend a church like this. God definitely wants that!

If you circled mostly _C_s, you are drawn to a more formal, even majestic kind of worship. The beauty of the sacrament of Communion appeals to you. You like the way it sounds so sacred. If you decide you'd like to visit a Lutheran or Episcopal or other "liturgical" church, and right now you go to an _A_-style church, you might meet a little resistance from your parents. _C_-style churches sometimes give the impression of being _too_ formal and rigid and of encouraging people to pay more attention to the ceremony than to God. That's just a perception. And it's almost certainly true of some people in _any_ style of church if they tend to be concerned with putting on a show rather than worshiping. You can share that with your parents, but if they say no, don't push it.

If God wants you to explore that option someday, he'll point you that way. If you do get to go, don't worry about whether you'll know what to do. It's all spelled out, and you won't find anything foreign there. After all, it's all about God—and you know him!

Girlz WANT TO KNOW

✿ _KRESHA: What about me? If my mom has to work on Sunday morning, I have to watch my little brothers and I don't get to go to church. That happens a lot. Does that mean I'm not worshiping? Isn't that bad?_

No, it's not bad, Kresha. It's just the way things are in your life right now, and you can't control that. Sure, it's important to worship with a church, but if you absolutely can't make it, there are other ways to worship. Make your Sunday quiet time special and include lots of praise.

Or the first time you have a chance (maybe when those little brothers are napping?), look out at something beautiful that God has created, even if it's just that pot of geraniums on the windowsill. Imagine God making them just to bless you. When your friends get home from church, call them and ask them to tell you all about the service. What was the sermon  about? Who in the congregation needs prayer this week? That way you'll feel connected. You might even share with them what you discovered in your private worship.

During the week see if there are other chances to worship that you *can* get to. Does your church have a Wednesday night service? Is there youth stuff happening on the weekend? Remember through it all that God understands your situation. Do your best. He's doing his.

Talking to God About It

Remember how Jesus said, "True worshipers will worship the Father in spirit and truth, for they are the kind of worshipers the Father seeks" (John 4:23)? Check out that term *seeks*. We've been talking through this whole chapter about what *we* are supposed to do to worship in spirit and truth—but Jesus said God the Father is also doing *his* thing. He's seeking worshipers. He's the one who's pulling us into worship. It's all his idea!

So instead of talking to God in our last prayer, let's listen.

Go to your usual quiet place, or choose a different one, or just get very still where you are right now. Close your eyes. Picture yourself sweeping any nagging thoughts over to a corner of your brain where you can come back to them later. Then put yourself in God's presence the way you've learned to do in this book. If that's still hard for you, just know that God is there, no matter what you do. You're just now paying attention. Tell God that you're open to anything he wants you to know in this moment. Then just listen. This is connection with God. This is worship.

If I could create a special worship service, here's what it would be like...

Chapter 1

I still say it's not fair."

Lily Robbins looked up from her suitcase at her younger sister, Tessa, who was letting both arms flop to the bed, over and over and over — and, oh yes, over. Lily knew Tessa would have been doing it with her legs if the body brace she was wearing had let her. It was what she did when she was afraid and wouldn't admit it.

"What are you scared of?" Lily said as she tried to cram one more Camp Galilee T-shirt into her already stuffed duffel bag.

"I'm not scared of nothin'," Tessa said, scowling. "I just said it ain't fair."

"Isn't fair."

"That's what I said!" The arms did a particularly hard flop. "It's not fair that I gotta stay here while you go to some dumb camp for two weeks."

Lily felt her lips twitch. "If it's dumb, why would you want to go anyway?"

Tessa's scowl deepened until Lily was sure her forehead was going to meet her chin. Nobody could scowl like Tessa.

"Besides," Lily said, "you're just now getting back on your feet since the accident. You'd have to sit and watch everybody else hike and rock climb and sail—" She stopped. Tessa's eyes were going into slits.

"Are you scared of being here without me?" Lily said.

"No, that's dumb."

"Are you scared you'll miss me so much you'll cry?"

"That's double dumb!"

Lily climbed on top of her duffel bag and squished it down while she pulled the zipper closed. The bulging sides puckered, and she could almost hear her clothes groaning. She swiveled to face Tessa, who was still trying to maintain the scowl. Lily could see her big green eyes misting up.

"Are you scared I'm not coming back or something?"

"No!" Tessa said. She slammed her arms down so hard that China, Lily's big stuffed panda, bounced two inches off the bed. Tessa turned her glare on him, so that all Lily could see was the wavy back of Tessa's short dark hair. "You're gonna forget about me while you're gone," she said. "That's what's gonna happen."

"No way!" Lily said. She scrambled up and sat next to Tessa on the bed. Otto, Lily's mutt dog, took that as his cue to join them and crawled out from under the bed and hopped up. Lily stroked his head and Tessa's at the same time. "I'm only gonna be gone two weeks," she said. "But even if I was gone the whole summer — or a whole *year* even — I wouldn't forget you. You're my sister."

"Adopted," Tessa muttered. "And I ain't even that yet. That dumb judge still has to make it — what's that word?"

"Official," Lily said. "But I don't need him to do that. You're my sister already, and I'm not gonna forget you, so quit talking like a freak."

Tessa turned to Lily and scoured her face with her eyes as if she were digging for traces of a lie. "Do you *wish* I was goin'?" she said.

"Well, yeah, du-uh!" Lily said. And she did. Tessa was still pretty rowdy and definitely stubborn, but she was nothing like the way she was when she'd first come to live with the Robbins family. Lily was having trouble imagining what it was going to be like not having Tessa tagging after her every minute, asking ten thousand questions. Tessa was what Dad called streetwise, but she didn't know a lot of stuff most nine-year-olds knew. Lily had taken it upon herself to teach her.

If I weren't so jazzed about this camp, Lily thought, *I'd stay home and help Mom and Dad work with her.* But her parents had urged her to go. They said they needed some one-on-one time with Tessa anyway — and Camp Galilee was the best Christian camp for girls in the whole eastern United States — or so everybody said. Mom and Dad were sure that if anybody would enjoy the special programs they had at Galilee, it was Lily.

Besides, the Girlz were all going — Reni and Suzy and Zooey and even Kresha. Their church had made sure Kresha got a scholarship since her mom didn't have a lot of money.

I have to spend all the time I can with my Girlz this summer, Lily thought. *The end of August is gonna be here before I know it, and then I won't see them for a whole year. A whole year!*

"You wanna go real bad," Tessa said. She was still studying Lily's face.

"Yeah, I do," Lily said. She had to be honest with Tessa. The kid had lie radar. "But I also wanna be with you. Too bad I can't be in two places at one time."

Otto gave a growl and wriggled away from Lily, squirming as close to Tessa's side as he could, and sighed himself in. So far, Tessa was the only other person in the Robbins family besides Lily that Otto would even allow to touch him. Ever since she had come home from the hospital, he had to be on the couch or the bed or the chair next to Tessa. The only exception was at night, when, as always, he crawled under Lily's covers like a mole and slept there.

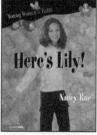

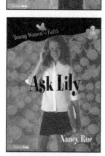

Young Women of Faith

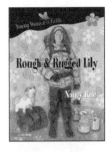
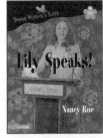

Rough & Rugged Lily (Book 9)
Softcover 0-310-70260-7
The Year 'Round Holiday Book companion

Lily Speaks! (Book 10)
Softcover 0-310-70262-3
The Values & Virtues Book companion

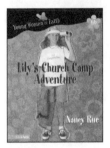

Horse Crazy Lily (Book 11)
Softcover 0-310-70263-1
The Fun-Finder Book companion

Lily's Church Camp Adventure (Book 12)
Softcover 0-310-70264-X
The Walk-the-Walk Book companion

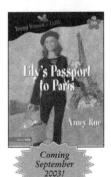

Lily's in London?! (Book 13)
Softcover 0-310-70554-1

Lily's Passport to Paris (Book 14)
Softcover 0-310-70555-X

Coming September 2003!

Coming September 2003!

Available now at your local bookstore!

Zonderkidz.

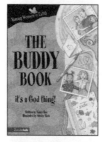

Young Women of Faith

The Year 'Round Holiday Book
... It's a God Thing!
Softcover 0-310-70256-9
Rough & Rugged Lily companion

The Values & Virtues Book
... It's a God Thing!
Softcover 0-310-70257-7
Lily Speaks! companion

The Fun-Finder Book
... It's a God Thing!
Softcover 0-310-70258-5
Horse Crazy Lily companion

The Walk-the-Walk Book
... It's a God Thing!
Softcover 0-310-70259-3
Lily's Church Camp Adventure companion

Available now at your local bookstore!

Zonderkidz.

NIV Young Women of Faith Bible
GENERAL EDITOR SUSIE SHELLENBERGER

Designed just for girls ages 8-12, the *NIV Young Women of Faith Bible* not only has a trendy, cool look, it's packed with fun to read in-text features that spark interest, provide insight, highlight key foundational portions of Scripture, and more. Discover how to apply God's word to your everyday life with the *NIV Young Women of Faith Bible.*

Hardcover 0-310-91394-2
Softcover 0-310-70278-X
Slate Leather–Look™ 0-310-70485-5
Periwinkle Leather–Look™ 0-310-70486-3

Available now at your local bookstore!

Zonderkidz.

We want to hear from you. Please send your comments about this
book to us in care of the address below. Thank you.

Zonder**kidz**™

Grand Rapids, MI 49530
www.zonderkidz.com